Copyright © 1987 by Kingfisher, Ltd.
First Edition in United States of America, 1987

Published in the United Kingdom under the
title THE KINGFISHER CHILDREN'S WORLD ATLAS

Printed in Italy by Vallardi Industrie Grafiche, Milan.

Library of Congress Cataloging-in-Publication Data

The Doubleday children's atlas.

    Includes index.
    Summary: Introduces the people, places, countries, and
continents of the world through relief maps, facts,
figures, and over 100 color photographs.
    1. Atlases. [1. Atlases. 2. Geography] I. Olliver,
Jane. II. Title. III. Title: Children's atlas.
G1021.D6 1987   912   86-675232
ISBN 0-385-24414-2

THE DOUBLEDAY
CHILDREN'S
ATLAS

Edited by Jane Olliver

Doubleday & Company, Inc.
Garden City, New York

Contents

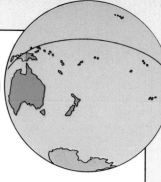

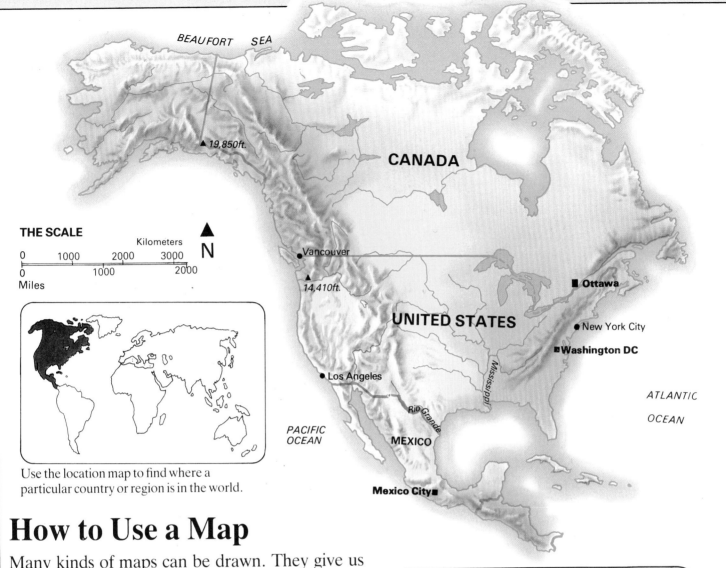

BEAUFORT SEA

CANADA

▲ 19,850ft.

THE SCALE

Kilometers
0   1000   2000   3000

N

0   1000   2000
Miles

● Vancouver

▲ 14,410ft.

UNITED STATES

■ **Ottawa**

● New York City

■**Washington DC**

Mississippi

● Los Angeles

Rio Grande

ATLANTIC

OCEAN

PACIFIC
OCEAN

MEXICO

Mexico City■

Use the location map to find where a
particular country or region is in the world.

How to Use a Map

Many kinds of maps can be drawn. They give us
different information. A *political* map, like the
one on pages 10–11, shows the boundaries of the
world's countries. The *physical* map on pages 12–
13 shows the land's surface with its oceans, rivers,
lakes, and mountains. Colors and *symbols* are
used on maps to give information. Look at the
map above. To see what the colors and symbols
mean, check the *key* on the right.

Maps are much smaller than the actual area of
the countries they show. But they are always
drawn to *scale*. Scale means the comparison
between the map size and the real size. If the scale
is written like this – 1:800,000, it means that one
inch on the map stands for 800,000 inches (12.5
miles) on the ground. The maps in this atlas have
a bar scale. You can measure any distance on the
map, then compare it to the bar scale to find the
real land distance.

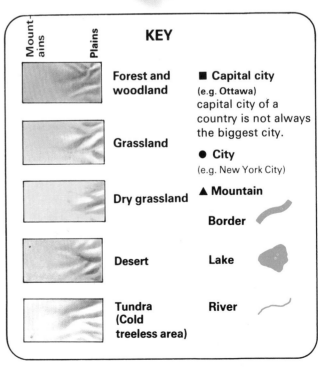

KEY

Mount-
ains

Plains

Forest and
woodland

Grassland

Dry grassland

Desert

Tundra
(Cold
treeless area)

■ **Capital city**
(e.g. Ottawa)
capital city of a
country is not always
the biggest city.

● **City**
(e.g. New York City)

▲ **Mountain**

Border

Lake

River

Maps and Mapmaking

Our earth is one of nine planets circling around the sun. It is the fifth-largest planet in the solar system. The earth is shaped like a ball. But it is slightly flattened at the top and bottom.

We can show the earth's land and seas as they are by drawing a map on the surface of a *globe*. A globe is a round ball, shaped like the earth. You can see a picture of a globe on the right. When it turns, we can see all the sides one by one. Look at these four views of the same globe.

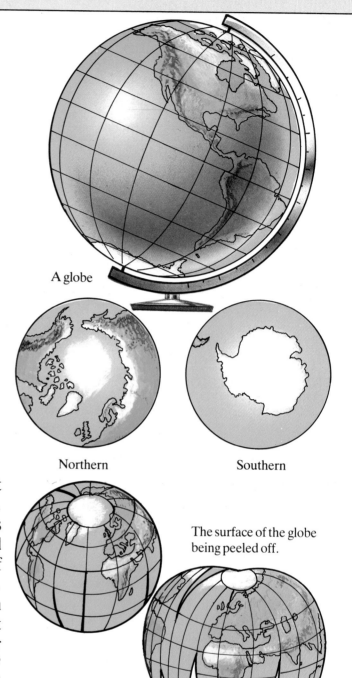

A globe

Western

Eastern

Northern

Southern

But if we want to show all the earth's sides at once on flat paper, we have to draw a *projection*. A projection is a flat drawing of rounded sections of the globe. It is impossible to lay a curved surface flat without twisting and pulling some of the sections. Try drawing a picture on an orange. Then peel the orange in segments and flatten them on a table. You will not be able to do it without squashing the peel out of shape, or *distorting* it. What has happened to your drawing? It is distorted. All maps of the world are distorted in one way or another.

The surface of the globe being peeled off.

The surface of the globe stretched flat.

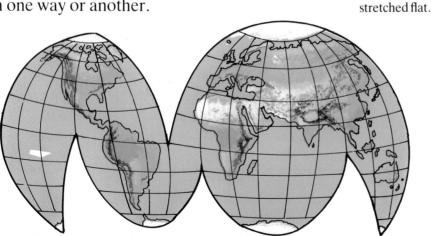

Above and left you can see one method of peeling the surface off a globe to make a flat map. The lines on the map running from north to south are lines of *longitude*. The lines running from east to west are the lines of *latitude*. These lines are very useful. Mapmakers use them to make sure that cities and boundaries are put in the right place on the map.

The Earth:
Facts and Figures

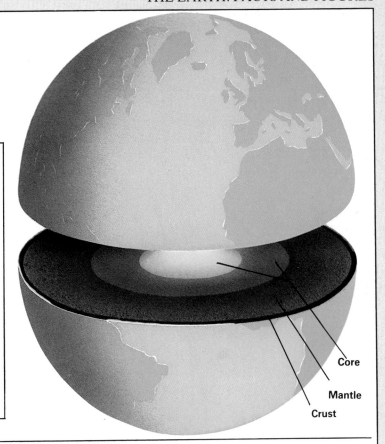

Core

Mantle

Crust

EARTH FACTS

Circumference around the equator: 24,902 miles.

Circumference around the poles: 24,860 miles.

Distance to center of earth: About 3,963.34 miles.

Surface area: About 197,751,000 square miles. Sea covers 71 percent of the surface of the earth.

Average distance from the sun: 93,000,000 miles. The earth is farther away from the sun in July than in January.

Rotation Speed: At the equator, the earth rotates on its axis at 1,032 miles per hour.

Speed in orbit: The earth travels at 18.5 miles per second.

Average distance from moon: 238,860 miles.

HIGHEST MOUNTAINS

	feet
Everest (Himalaya-Nepal/Tibet)	29,028
Godwin Austen (Pakistan/India)	28,250
Kanchenjunga (Himalaya-Nepal/Sikkim)	28,208
Makalu (Himalaya-Nepal/Tibet)	27,824
Dhaulagiri (Himalaya-Nepal)	26,810
Nanga Parbat (Himalaya-India)	26,660
Annapurna (Himalaya-Nepal)	26,504
Communism Peak (U.S.S.R.)	24,590
Aconcagua (Andes-Argentina)	22,831
McKinley (Alaska)	20,320
Kilimanjaro (Tanzania)	19,340
Elbrus (Caucasus-U.S.S.R.)	18,510

LONGEST RIVERS

	miles
Nile (Africa)	4,145
Amazon (S. America)	3,915
Yangtze (China)	3,910
Mississippi-Missouri-Red Rock (N. America)	3,741
Ob-Irtysh (U.S.S.R.)	3,362
Yenisei (U.S.S.R.)	3,100
Hwang Ho	2,877
Amur (Asia)	2,744
Lena (U.S.S.R.)	2,734
Zaire* (Africa)	2,718
Mackenzie-Peace-Finlay (Canada)	2,635
Mekong (S.E. Asia)	2,610
Niger (Africa)	2,548

*Formerly Congo River

LARGEST ISLANDS

	square miles
Greenland	840,000
New Guinea	305,000
Borneo	290,000
Madagascar	226,400
Baffin I.	195,928
Sumatra	164,000
Honshu	88,000
Great Britain	84,400
Victoria I.	83,896
Ellesmere	75,767

OCEANS

	square miles
Pacific	61,186,000
Atlantic	31,862,000
Indian	28,350,000
Arctic	5,427,000

The highest waterfall is part of the Angel Falls, Venezuela.

MAJOR WATERFALLS

Highest	feet
Angel Falls (Venezuela)	3,212
Tugela Falls (South Africa)	3,110
Yosemite Falls (California)	2,425

Greatest volume	cubic feet per second
Niagara (N. America)	212,000

DESERTS

	square miles
Sahara	3,243,500
Australian Desert	600,000
Arabian Desert	520,000
Gobi	402,000
Kalahari	200,000

LARGEST LAKES

	square miles
Caspian Sea (U.S.S.R./Iran)	143,243
Superior (U.S.A./Canada)	31,820
Victoria Nyanza (Africa)	26,724
Aral (U.S.S.R.)	25,676
Huron (U.S.A./Canada)	23,010
Michigan (U.S.A.)	22,400
Tanganyika (Africa)	12,650
Baikal (U.S.S.R.)	12,162
Great Bear (Canada)	12,096
Malawi* (Africa)	11,555
Great Slave Lake (Canada)	11,031

*Also called Lake Nyasa

The highest mountain is the peak of Everest above Khumbu glacier.

The largest desert is the Sahara, which stretches across northern Africa.

Greenland

Alaska

ICELAND

C A N A D A

UNITED KINGDOM

IRELAND

FRANCE

7

SPAIN

PORTUGAL

25

MOROCCO

U N I T E D   S T A T E S
O F   A M E R I C A

ALGERIA

TROPIC OF CANCER

MEXICO

BAHAMAS

MAURITANIA

MALI

CUBA

CAPE
VERDE
ISLANDS

46

53

56

26

54   55

DOMINICA
ST LUCIA
BARBADOS

27

28

29

48

57

30

GHANA

50

52

31

47

VENEZUELA

32

49

33

51

58

IVORY COAST

59 60

COLOMBIA

35

EQUATOR

ECUADOR

PERU

BRAZIL

TROPIC OF CAPRICORN

BOLIVIA

PARAGUAY

URUGUAY

C H I L E

ARGENTINA

Falkland Islands

1 DENMARK	**11** YUGOSLAVIA	
2 NETHERLANDS	**12** ALBANIA	
3 BELGIUM	**13** CYPRUS	
4 LUXEMBOURG	**14** LEBANON	
5 W. GERMANY	**15** ISRAEL	
6 E. GERMANY	**16** SYRIA	
7 SWITZERLAND	**17** JORDAN	
8 AUSTRIA	**18** KUWAIT	
9 CZECHOSLOVAKIA	**19** BAHRAIN	
10 HUNGARY	**20** UNITED ARAB EMIRATES	

Countries of the World

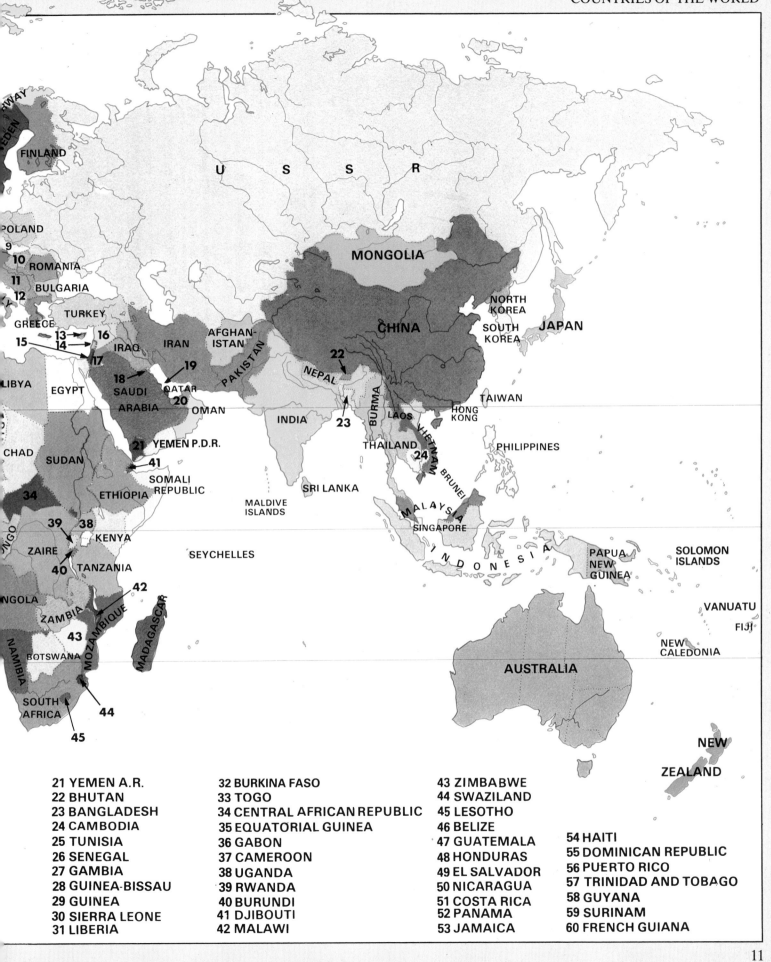

RWAY
SWEDEN
FINLAND
POLAND
9
10 ROMANIA
11 BULGARIA
12
GREECE
TURKEY
15 13 16
14 17
LIBYA
EGYPT
IRAQ
IRAN
AFGHAN-ISTAN
18 QATAR
19
SAUDI ARABIA
20 OMAN
PAKISTAN
NEPAL
22
23
INDIA
21 YEMEN P.D.R.
41
CHAD
SUDAN
34
SOMALI REPUBLIC
ETHIOPIA
39 38
ZAIRE
KENYA
NGO
40 TANZANIA
NGOLA
ZAMBIA
42
43
NAMIBIA
BOTSWANA
MADAGASCAR
MOZAMBIQUE
SOUTH AFRICA
44
45

U S S R
MONGOLIA
CHINA
NORTH KOREA
SOUTH KOREA
JAPAN
TAIWAN
BURMA
LAOS
HONG KONG
THAILAND
VIETNAM
24
BRUNEI
MALAYSIA
SINGAPORE
PHILIPPINES
SRI LANKA
MALDIVE ISLANDS
SEYCHELLES
I N D O N E S I A
PAPUA NEW GUINEA
SOLOMON ISLANDS
VANUATU
FIJI
NEW CALEDONIA
AUSTRALIA
NEW ZEALAND

21 YEMEN A.R.	32 BURKINA FASO	43 ZIMBABWE
22 BHUTAN	33 TOGO	44 SWAZILAND
23 BANGLADESH	34 CENTRAL AFRICAN REPUBLIC	45 LESOTHO
24 CAMBODIA	35 EQUATORIAL GUINEA	46 BELIZE
25 TUNISIA	36 GABON	47 GUATEMALA
26 SENEGAL	37 CAMEROON	48 HONDURAS
27 GAMBIA	38 UGANDA	49 EL SALVADOR
28 GUINEA-BISSAU	39 RWANDA	50 NICARAGUA
29 GUINEA	40 BURUNDI	51 COSTA RICA
30 SIERRA LEONE	41 DJIBOUTI	52 PANAMA
31 LIBERIA	42 MALAWI	53 JAMAICA

54 HAITI
55 DOMINICAN REPUBLIC
56 PUERTO RICO
57 TRINIDAD AND TOBAGO
58 GUYANA
59 SURINAM
60 FRENCH GUIANA

The Continents

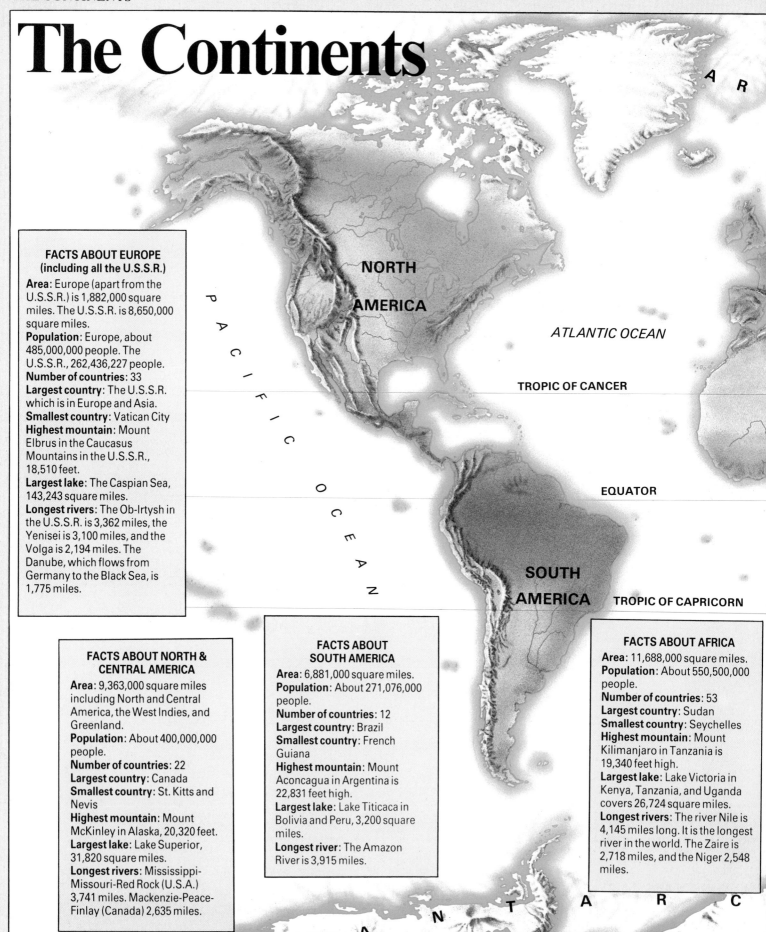

NORTH

AMERICA

ATLANTIC OCEAN

P
A
C
I
F
I
C

O
C
E
A
N

TROPIC OF CANCER

EQUATOR

SOUTH

AMERICA   TROPIC OF CAPRICORN

A   R

A   N   T   A   R   C

FACTS ABOUT EUROPE
(including all the U.S.S.R.)

Area: Europe (apart from the U.S.S.R.) is 1,882,000 square miles. The U.S.S.R. is 8,650,000 square miles.

Population: Europe, about 485,000,000 people. The U.S.S.R., 262,436,227 people.

Number of countries: 33

Largest country: The U.S.S.R. which is in Europe and Asia.

Smallest country: Vatican City

Highest mountain: Mount Elbrus in the Caucasus Mountains in the U.S.S.R., 18,510 feet.

Largest lake: The Caspian Sea, 143,243 square miles.

Longest rivers: The Ob-Irtysh in the U.S.S.R. is 3,362 miles, the Yenisei is 3,100 miles, and the Volga is 2,194 miles. The Danube, which flows from Germany to the Black Sea, is 1,775 miles.

FACTS ABOUT NORTH & CENTRAL AMERICA

Area: 9,363,000 square miles including North and Central America, the West Indies, and Greenland.

Population: About 400,000,000 people.

Number of countries: 22

Largest country: Canada

Smallest country: St. Kitts and Nevis

Highest mountain: Mount McKinley in Alaska, 20,320 feet.

Largest lake: Lake Superior, 31,820 square miles.

Longest rivers: Mississippi-Missouri-Red Rock (U.S.A.) 3,741 miles. Mackenzie-Peace-Finlay (Canada) 2,635 miles.

FACTS ABOUT SOUTH AMERICA

Area: 6,881,000 square miles.

Population: About 271,076,000 people.

Number of countries: 12

Largest country: Brazil

Smallest country: French Guiana

Highest mountain: Mount Aconcagua in Argentina is 22,831 feet high.

Largest lake: Lake Titicaca in Bolivia and Peru, 3,200 square miles.

Longest river: The Amazon River is 3,915 miles.

FACTS ABOUT AFRICA

Area: 11,688,000 square miles.

Population: About 550,500,000 people.

Number of countries: 53

Largest country: Sudan

Smallest country: Seychelles

Highest mountain: Mount Kilimanjaro in Tanzania is 19,340 feet high.

Largest lake: Lake Victoria in Kenya, Tanzania, and Uganda covers 26,724 square miles.

Longest rivers: The river Nile is 4,145 miles long. It is the longest river in the world. The Zaire is 2,718 miles, and the Niger 2,548 miles.

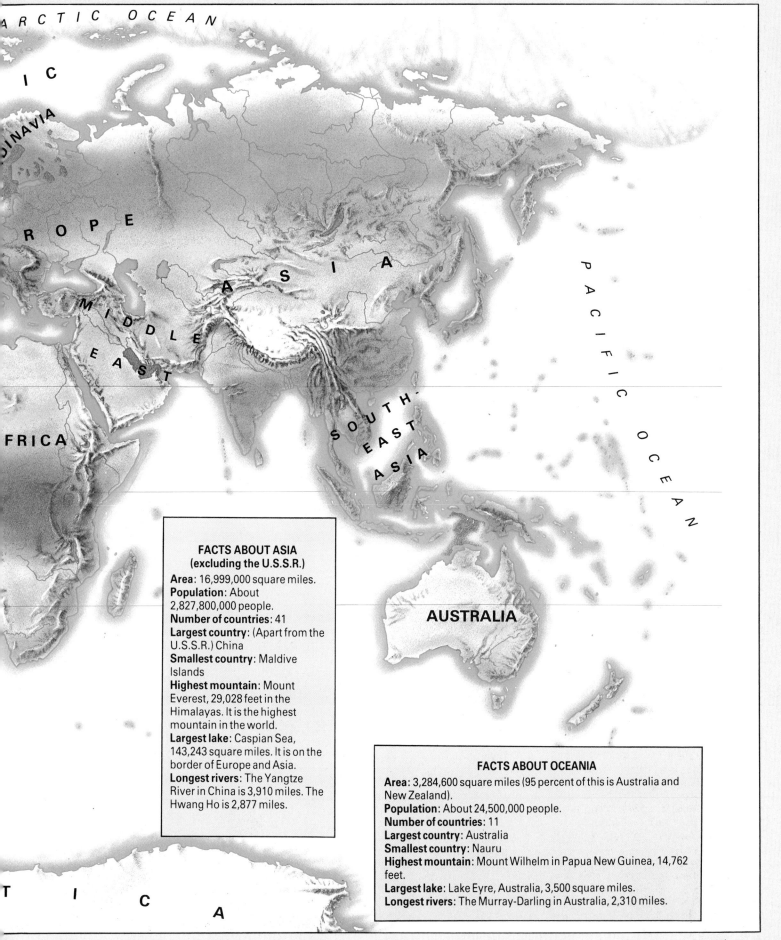

ARCTIC OCEAN

IC

DINAVIA

ROPE

MIDDLE

EAST

ASIA

FRICA

SOUTH-
EAST
ASIA

PACIFIC OCEAN

AUSTRALIA

TICA

FACTS ABOUT ASIA
(excluding the U.S.S.R.)
Area: 16,999,000 square miles.
Population: About
2,827,800,000 people.
Number of countries: 41
Largest country: (Apart from the
U.S.S.R.) China
Smallest country: Maldive
Islands
Highest mountain: Mount
Everest, 29,028 feet in the
Himalayas. It is the highest
mountain in the world.
Largest lake: Caspian Sea,
143,243 square miles. It is on the
border of Europe and Asia.
Longest rivers: The Yangtze
River in China is 3,910 miles. The
Hwang Ho is 2,877 miles.

FACTS ABOUT OCEANIA
Area: 3,284,600 square miles (95 percent of this is Australia and
New Zealand).
Population: About 24,500,000 people.
Number of countries: 11
Largest country: Australia
Smallest country: Nauru
Highest mountain: Mount Wilhelm in Papua New Guinea, 14,762
feet.
Largest lake: Lake Eyre, Australia, 3,500 square miles.
Longest rivers: The Murray-Darling in Australia, 2,310 miles.

Scandinavia and Finland

Thousands of years ago Scandinavia was covered with ice sheets and glaciers. These cut deep *fjords* into the coastline and formed many lakes and islands. Iceland is the most northern country in Europe. It still has many snowfields. It is also dotted with many hot springs, steaming geysers and over a hundred volcanoes.

Most Scandinavians enjoy a high standard of living. Sweden is the largest and richest of the countries. Over half the Swedish people live in modern cities, such as Stockholm and Göteborg. Many earn their living by manufacturing paper and other wood products. Sweden, Norway, and Finland have large areas of forest.

Scandinavia's coastal waters teem with fish. Fishermen, mainly from Iceland and Norway, catch large quantities of cod and herring, which are canned or frozen in fish-processing factories.

Dairy farming is important in Denmark. Only one fifth of the people are farmers, but they use the latest machinery and farming methods.

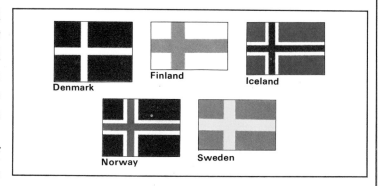

Denmark   Finland   Iceland   Norway   Sweden

Above: The Copenhagen waterfront is very busy. Fishing, shipping, and tourism are important industries in Denmark.

Left: There are hundreds of fjords in Norway. The force of the water falling down cliffs is used to make electricity.

Right: The sculpture in Copenhagen harbor is called the *Little Mermaid* after the fairy tale by Hans Christian Andersen.

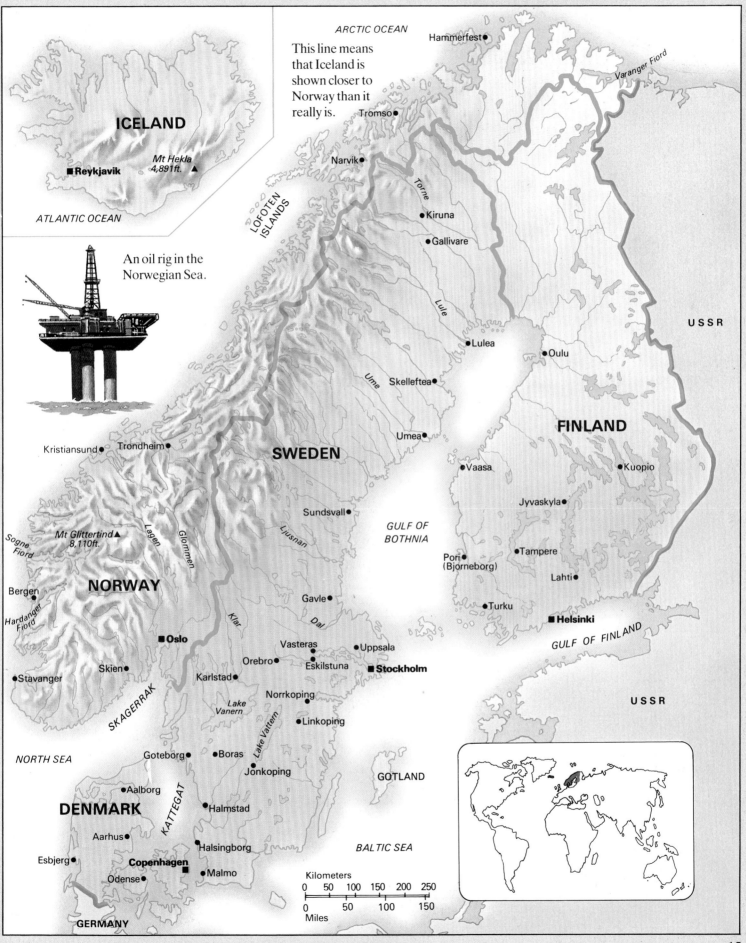

ARCTIC OCEAN

Hammerfest•

Varanger Fiord

This line means
that Iceland is
shown closer to
Norway than it
really is.

Tromso•

ICELAND

Mt Hekla
4,891ft. ▲

■ **Reykjavik**

ATLANTIC OCEAN

An oil rig in the
Norwegian Sea.

*LOFOTEN
ISLANDS*

Narvik•

Torne

•Kiruna

•Gallivare

Lule

•Lulea

Oulu•

U S S R

Skelleftea•

Kristiansund•   •Trondheim

SWEDEN

Umea•

FINLAND

•Vaasa

•Kuopio

*Sogne
Fiord*

Mt Glittertind▲
8,110ft.

Lagen

Glommen

Sundsvall•

Jyvaskyla•

•Tampere

Ljusnan

**GULF OF
BOTHNIA**

Pori•
(Bjorneborg)

Lahti•

Bergen•

NORWAY

Klar

Dal

Gavle•

•Turku

■ **Helsinki**

*Hardanger
Fiord*

Skien•

■ **Oslo**

Vasteras•   •Uppsala

GULF OF FINLAND

•Stavanger

Karlstad•

Orebro•   Eskilstuna•   ■ **Stockholm**

U S S R

SKAGERRAK

Norrkoping•

*Lake
Vanern*

•Linkoping

Lake Vattern

NORTH SEA

Goteborg•   •Boras

GOTLAND

•Aalborg

Jonkoping•

DENMARK

KATTEGAT

Halmstad•

Aarhus•

Halsingborg•

BALTIC SEA

Esbjerg•   **Copenhagen**■

•Malmo

Odense•

Kilometers
0 50 100 150 200 250

0   50   100   150
Miles

GERMANY

Netherlands, Belgium, and Luxembourg

Netherlands Belgium Luxembourg

The Netherlands, Belgium, and Luxembourg are known as the Low Countries because much of the land is flat and below sea level. In the Netherlands high *dikes*, or sea walls, have been built around low-lying lands, which are called *polders*. Nearly a quarter of the Netherlands' land has been *reclaimed*, or taken back, from the sea in this way.

The Low Countries have a combined population of nearly 25 million. This makes them the most densely populated group of countries in Europe. They are also wealthy countries. Most people work in offices and factories, often in textile and electrical companies. Others work on the land. The farms are small and very modern. Dutch farmers grow either flowers or vegetables or keep cows. There are also large iron and steel mills in Belgium and Luxembourg. Luxembourgers are *bilingual*. They speak two languages—French and Luxemburgish.

Below left: A flower market and many beautiful old buildings can be found in the Grand Place of Brussels. Brussels is the headquarters of the Common Market (E.E.C.).

Below: Windmills are often seen in the Dutch countryside. They were once used to pump water from polders to stop flooding.

Cheeses like Edam and Gouda are made in the Netherlands. They are sold in cheese markets.

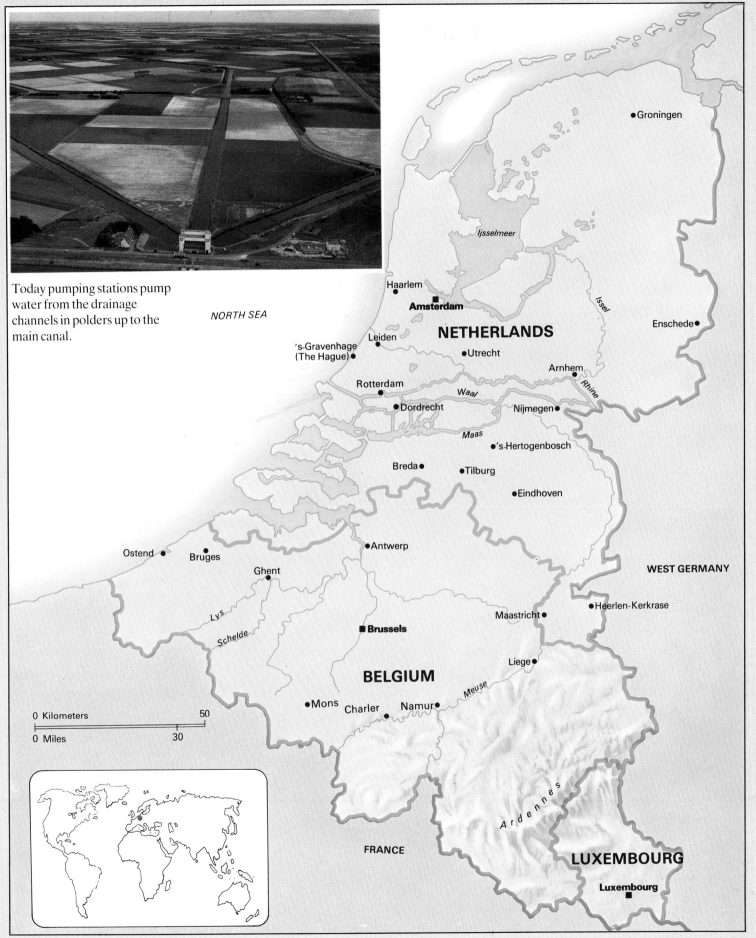

Today pumping stations pump water from the drainage channels in polders up to the main canal.

NORTH SEA

Groningen

Ijsselmeer

Haarlem

Amsterdam

NETHERLANDS

Issel

Enschede

Leiden

's-Gravenhage
(The Hague)

Utrecht

Arnhem

Rhine

Rotterdam

Waal

Dordrecht

Nijmegen

Maas

's-Hertogenbosch

Breda

Tilburg

Eindhoven

WEST GERMANY

Ostend

Bruges

Antwerp

Ghent

Heerlen-Kerkrase

Lys

Maastricht

Brussels

Schelde

Liege

BELGIUM

Meuse

0 Kilometers 50

0 Miles 30

Mons

Charler

Namur

Ardennes

FRANCE

LUXEMBOURG

Luxembourg

The British Isles

The British Isles is made up of two countries: the United Kingdom and the Republic of Ireland. The United Kingdom consists of Great Britain (England, Wales, and Scotland) and Northern Ireland. Many people call the United Kingdom simply Britain. The Republic of Ireland or Eire was once part of the United Kingdom. But in 1921 it became a separate country.

A moist climate makes Britain and the Republic of Ireland ideal for farming. But in Britain one third of the food must still be *imported*, or bought from other countries. The farms are too small to feed the large population.

Industry is very important in Britain. For every one person working on the land, there are ten people living and working in cities. Britain pays for the food it imports by selling manufactured products, such as cars, to other countries.

Britain is divided into many different districts with their own customs and *dialects*, or ways of speaking. In Wales children learn Welsh as well as English in schools.

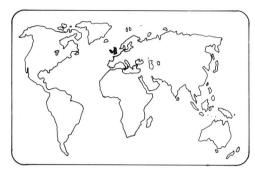

United Kingdom

Ireland

Above: The Houses of Parliament stand beside the river Thames in London. London is the capital of the United Kingdom.

Left: Fishguard is on the coast of south Wales. Most Welsh people live in cities in the south because the north is mountainous.

Below: Eilean Donan Castle is in northwest Scotland.

ORKNEY
ISLANDS

SHETLAND ISLANDS

*John o'
Groats*

Loch Ness *Dee*
• Inverness

• Aberdeen

▲ *Ben Nevis
1347m*

Grampians

HEBRIDES

Northwest Highlands

Oban • SCOTLAND Dundee •
  Tay • Perth

*Loch
Lomond* • Dunfermline

Glasgow • • Edinburgh
  Clyde

• Ayr

A Scottish trawler

An oil-rig explores the
British oil field in the
North Sea.

• Londonderry

NORTHERN
IRELAND

Belfast •

Tyne

Pennines

Eden

Newcastle •
• Sunderland

Lake
District

• Middlesbrough
and Teesside

*N O R T H

S E A*

• Sligo

ISLE OF MAN

• York

*Lough
Mask*

Blackpool • • Bradford • Leeds Hull •

Central Plains
• Galway

Dublin ■

*I R I S H

S E A*

Manchester •

Liverpool • • Sheffield

Shannon *Lough
Derg* *Wicklow
Mts*

▲ *Snowdon
1086m* *Trent*

Nottingham •
• Stoke-on-Trent

REPUBLIC OF
IRELAND (EIRE)

Barrow

Cambrian Mts

• Wolverhampton
Dudley • • Walsall
  Birmingham • Leicester •

*The
Fens*

• Great
Yarmouth
Norwich •

*Mts of
Kerry*

• Waterford

• Coventry

Ouse • Cambridge

Bedford •

• Ipswich

• Cork

Fishguard •

WALES

Severn

ENGLAND

Avon
Cotswolds

Oxford •

Chiltern Hills

London ■

• Swansea

Thames

Cardiff •

Bristol •
Bath •

North Downs • Canterbury

A T L A N T I C

O C E A N

Exmoor

Southampton • • Portsmouth

• Dover

Exeter •
Dartmoor

Bournemouth •

• Brighton
• Eastbourne

Isle of Wight

Plymouth •

*Land's
End*

ISLES OF
SCILLY

E N G L I S H C H A N N E L

Kilometers
0 20 40 60 80 100

0   25   50
Miles

FRANCE

CHANNEL ISLANDS

19

France

France is the largest country in Europe, except for the U.S.S.R. Along most of its borders there are mountain ranges. The Jura Mountains separate France from Switzerland, the Pyrenees separate it from Spain, and the Vosges separate France partly from Germany. The Alps border France with Italy and contain Mont Blanc, which is the highest peak in France.

Although many French people work in factories, farming is very important. The warm climate and rich soil help farmers to grow cereals, fruit, and sugar beet. Grapes, used for making wine, are grown in most regions. But the main grapevine growing areas are in Bordeaux, Burgundy, and Champagne. Dairy farming is also important and over 300 different cheeses are made.

Paris, Lyon, and Marseille are the main cities in France. Painters and writers from all over the world have lived in Paris. Many tourists go there today to see its historic buildings, which include the Louvre, the Notre Dame cathedral, and the Eiffel Tower.

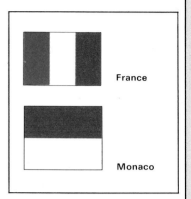

France

Monaco

Workers making Renault cars in a huge factory near Paris.

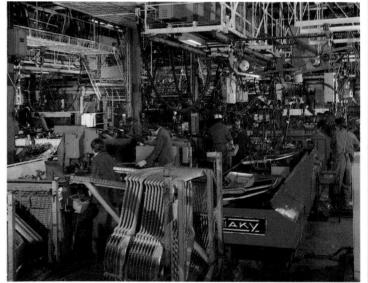

The Eiffel Tower was built in 1889 for the Great Exhibition. It is made of iron and is 1,312 feet high. A spectacular view of Paris can be seen from the higher levels of the tower.

The beautiful Chateau de Chenonceaux is in the Loire Valley. Moats were built around many chateaux to protect them from invaders.

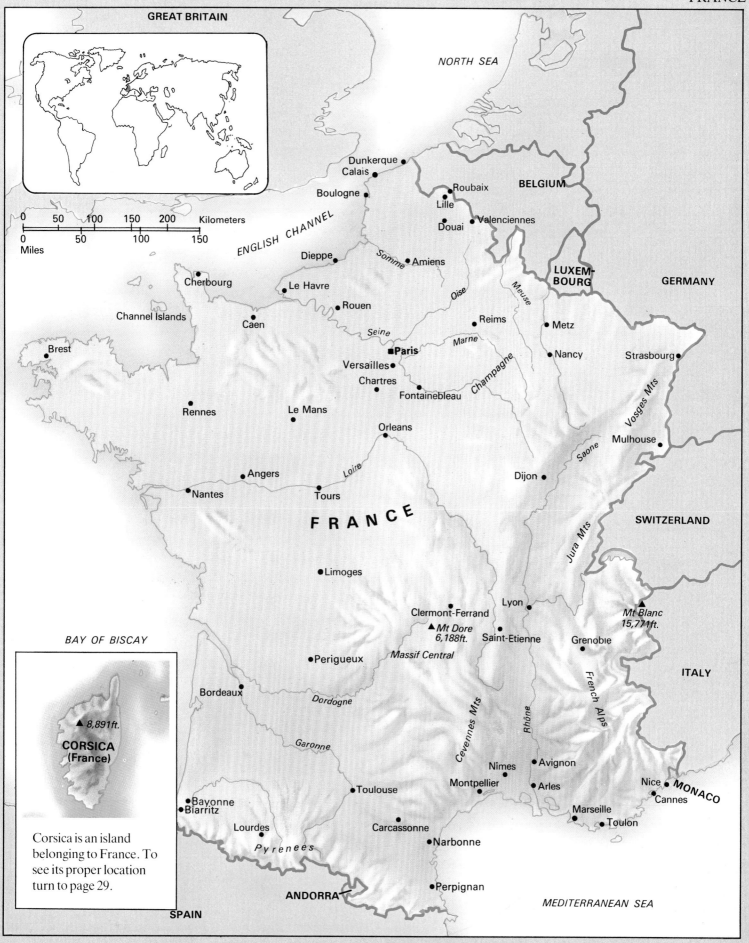

GREAT BRITAIN

NORTH SEA

BELGIUM

LUXEM-
BOURG

GERMANY

Kilometers

0   50   100   150   200   Kilometers

0   50   100   150   Miles
Miles

ENGLISH CHANNEL

Dunkerque
Calais
Boulogne
Roubaix
Lille
Douai
Valenciennes

Dieppe
Somme
Amiens

Cherbourg
Le Havre
Oise
Meuse

Rouen
Reims
Metz

Channel Islands
Caen
Seine
Marne
Nancy
Strasbourg

Brest
Paris
Champagne

Versailles
Chartres
Fontainebleau

Vosges Mts

Rennes
Le Mans

Orleans
Mulhouse

Loire
Saone

Angers
Dijon

Nantes
Tours

F R A N C E

SWITZERLAND

Jura Mts

Limoges

Lyon

Mt Blanc
15,771ft.

Clermont-Ferrand
▲ Mt Dore
6,188ft.
Saint-Etienne
Grenoble

Perigueux
Massif Central

ITALY

Bordeaux
Dordogne

French Alps

BAY OF BISCAY

Garonne

Cevennes Mts

Rhône

Avignon

Nimes
Montpellier
Arles
Nice
MONACO
Cannes

▲ 8,891ft.

CORSICA
(France)

Toulouse

Marseille
Toulon

Bayonne
Biarritz

Carcassonne

Lourdes

Narbonne

Corsica is an island
belonging to France. To
see its proper location
turn to page 29.

P y r e n e e s

Perpignan

MEDITERRANEAN SEA

ANDORRA

SPAIN

Germany: West and East

Since 1945 Germany has been divided into West Germany and East Germany. West Germany's proper name is the Federal Republic of Germany. East Germany's proper name is the German Democratic Republic. The city of Berlin is also divided into east and west *zones*. In 1961 a wall was built along East Berlin's boundaries to stop people crossing into West Germany.

The Germans are well-organized and hard-working people. Since 1945 large numbers of factories have been set up in both East and West Germany. These manufacture everything from steel to textiles. In West Germany workers in the industrial Ruhr Valley make cars, heavy machinery, cables, and electrical equipment. Today West Germany is one of the wealthiest countries in Europe.

Farming as well as manufacturing is important in East Germany. There are also many *lignite* mines. Lignite is a type of coal. East Germany is the world's chief supplier of lignite. Workers mine around 250 million tons of it every year.

West Germany

East Germany

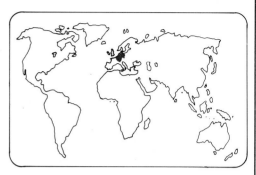

Above: Hamburg is a major docking point in the North Sea.

Left: Before the Berlin Wall was built, the Brandenburg Gate was the main thoroughfare between East and West Berlin.

Below: Barges travel down the Rhine in West Germany past lovely towns and castles, green fields, and vineyards.

ACHTUNG!
Sie verlassen jetzt
WEST-BERLIN

Kilometers
0   50   100   150
0   30   60   90
Miles

NORTH SEA

Kiel Canal

Kiel

Rostock

Lubeck

Hamburg

Elbe

POLAND

Bremen

Oder

Aller

Weser

Hanover

Brunswick

Magdeburg

Berlin

EAST GERMANY

Oder

NETHERLANDS

Munster

Bielefeld

Harz Mts

Spree

Rhine

Dortmund

Essen   Bochum

Duisburg

Ruhr

Kassel

Halle

Elbe

Krefeld   Wuppertal

Monchen-gladbach   Dusseldorf

Cologne

Leipzig

Aachen

Bonn

Dresden

Karl-Marx-Stadt

WEST GERMANY

BELGIUM

Mosel

Wiesbaden   Frankfurt

Mainz

Main

CZECHOSLOVAKIA

LUXEMBOURG

Mannheim

Nuremberg

Saarbrucken

Rhine

Karlsruhe

Stuttgart

Danube

Black Forest

FRANCE

Augsburg

Munich

AUSTRIA

SWITZERLAND

Switzerland and Austria

Switzerland and Austria are well known for their snowcapped mountains called the Alps. The Alps attract many visitors who like to ski in the winter and visit lakes, glaciers, and alpine meadows full of wild flowers in the summer. Long tunnels and bridges take roads and railroads through the mountains and valleys.

In Switzerland rivers are dammed to catch water and make electricity for homes and factories. This is called *hydroelectricity*. Many Swiss people work in factories making chemicals, scientific instruments, clocks and watches, and delicious chocolate. Banks and hotels provide important jobs.

Most Swiss people speak German, but French, Italian, and Romansch are also spoken.

Austria was part of a large and important country called the Austro-Hungarian Empire until 1918. Now it is quite small. Austria has some minerals such as iron and oil, but tourism is also very important. Most Austrians live in towns. Vienna, the capital, is famous for its music. In the past famous musicians such as Beethoven and Mozart have lived and composed music there.

Sandwiched between Austria and Switzerland is the tiny country of Liechtenstein.

Holiday resorts in Switzerland are well known for their fresh mountain air and clear lakes. In the summer, boating and mountain climbing are popular activities.

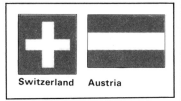
Switzerland Austria

Left: Among the many large lakes in Switzerland is Lake Luzern.

Right: Ice skating out of doors is possible for many months in alpine countries.

Below: An outdoor cafe in a busy Vienna shopping district provides a meeting place for friends.

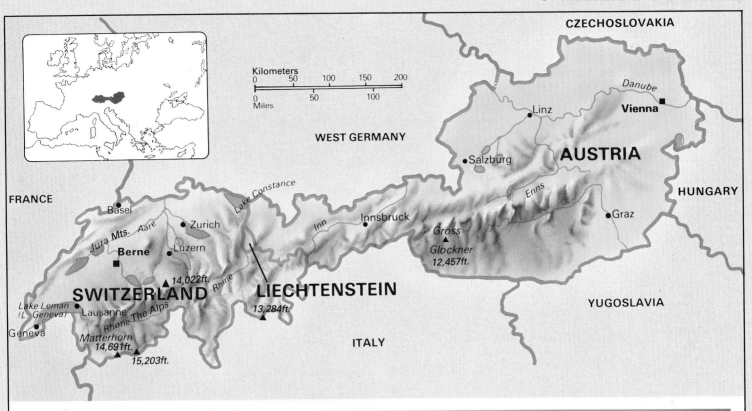

CZECHOSLOVAKIA

Danube

Vienna

Linz

AUSTRIA

Salzburg

HUNGARY

Enns

WEST GERMANY

Graz

Lake Constance

Innsbruck

Inn

Gross Glockner
12,457ft.

FRANCE

Basel

Jura Mts. *Aare*

Zurich

Berne

Luzern

Rhine

14,022ft.

SWITZERLAND

YUGOSLAVIA

LIECHTENSTEIN

13,284ft.

Lausanne

*Lake Leman
(L. Geneva)*

Rhone *The Alps*

ITALY

Geneva

Matterhorn
14,691ft.

15,203ft.

Spain and Portugal

Spain's interior is a vast *plateau*, which means an area of high flat ground. It is crossed by several mountain ranges. But the highest peaks are in the Pyrenees in the north and the Sierra Nevada in the south. Fertile plains and sandy beaches surround the central plateau. Spain is divided into several regions. One of these is Andalusia in the south. It is famous for its lively fiestas and gypsy flamenco dancers.

Spain's warm climate and golden sands attract thousands of tourists to its coastal resorts. Many Spaniards work in the tourist industry, but most work on the land. Some farmers do everything by hand or with the help of a donkey or mule. The soil is very dry and needs to be constantly watered, or *irrigated*. Farmers grow wheat, rice, olives, grapes, and oranges.

Spain

Portugal

Andorra

Top: Roman walls surround a city in Castile, a region in central Spain. The Romans ruled in Spain for six hundred years.

Middle: Workers in Portugal gather bark from cork trees to make cork.

Far left: Tourists relax on the warm, sunny beaches of Ibiza.

Left: A fisherman mends his net in Albufeira, Portugal. Huge numbers of sardines are caught off Portugal's coast.

Portugal borders Spain on the west. Most people are fishermen and farmers. Others work in the tourist industry or in factories where they process food and make textiles. There are large cork forests in Portugal and many vineyards. Cork and port, a special type of wine, are exported to countries all over the world.

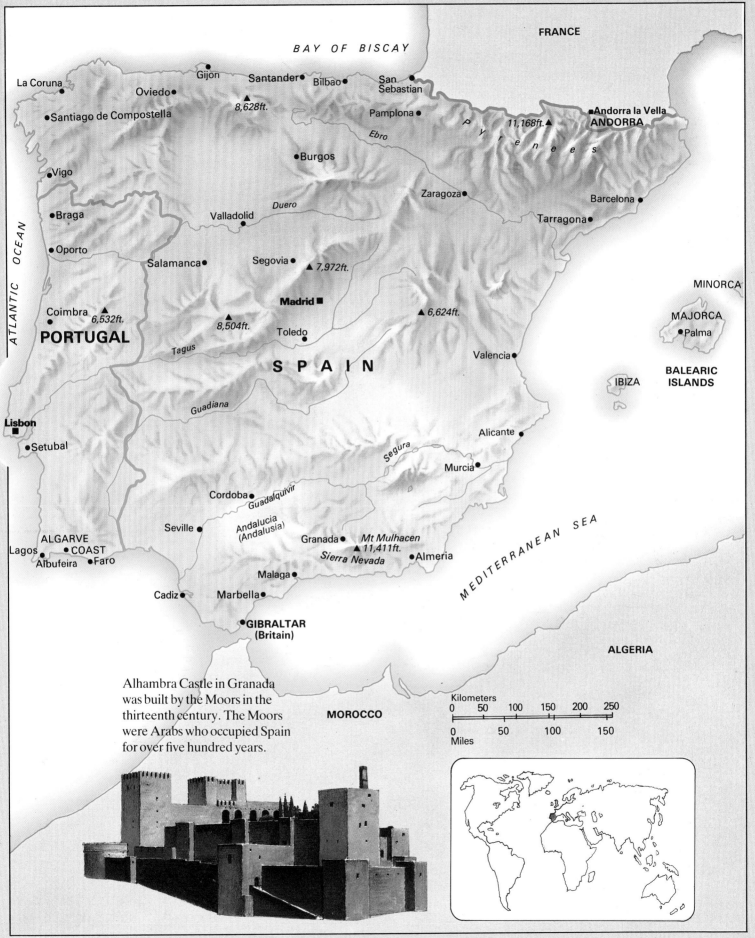

FRANCE

BAY OF BISCAY

ATLANTIC OCEAN

La Coruna
Gijon
Santander • Bilbao
San Sebastian
Oviedo
Santiago de Compostella
8,628ft.
Pamplona
Pyrenees
11,168ft. ▲
Andorra la Vella
ANDORRA
Ebro
Vigo
Burgos
Zaragoza
Barcelona
Braga
Valladolid
Duero
Tarragona
Oporto
Salamanca
Segovia ▲ 7,972ft.
MINORCA
Madrid ■
MAJORCA
Palma
Coimbra ▲ 6,532ft.
8,504ft. ▲
▲ 6,624ft.
PORTUGAL
Toledo
SPAIN
Valencia
BALEARIC ISLANDS
Tagus
IBIZA
Guadiana
Lisbon
Setubal
Segura
Alicante
Murcia
Cordoba
Guadalquivir
MEDITERRANEAN SEA
ALGARVE
Lagos • COAST
Albufeira • Faro
Seville
Andalucia (Andalusia)
Granada
Mt Mulhacen ▲ 11,411ft.
Sierra Nevada
Almeria
Malaga
Cadiz
Marbella
GIBRALTAR (Britain)

ALGERIA

Alhambra Castle in Granada was built by the Moors in the thirteenth century. The Moors were Arabs who occupied Spain for over five hundred years.

MOROCCO

Kilometers
0 50 100 150 200 250
0 50 100 150
Miles

Italy and Its Neighbors

Italy is shaped like a boot kicking a ball. Sicily is the "ball." Sicily, Sardinia, and many smaller islands are also part of Italy. The Apennine Mountains run down the back of Italy like a spine. There are several volcanic mountains in Italy. The best known is Mount Vesuvius, near the city of Naples in southern Italy.

Tourists flock to Italy to enjoy the warm climate, to see the beautiful buildings and paintings, and to visit the ruins of ancient Rome. In the north there are large industrial cities, such as Milan and Turin. Italians make textiles and cars for *export*, to sell to other countries. In the south farmers grow olives, citrus fruit, and grapes for making wine.

Vatican City is the smallest country in Europe. It is the home of the Pope, the head of the Roman Catholic Church. San Marino is another tiny country in Italy and Malta is an island country in the Mediterranean Sea.

Italy

San Marino

Vatican City

Malta

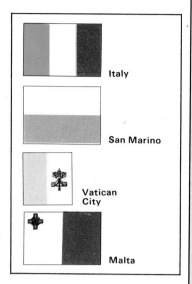

Above: St. Peter's Square is in Vatican City.
Left: Venice has many fine churches like Santa Maria della Salute. Boats called *gondolas* take people from place to place on canals that run through the city.
Right: The Leaning Tower of Pisa.

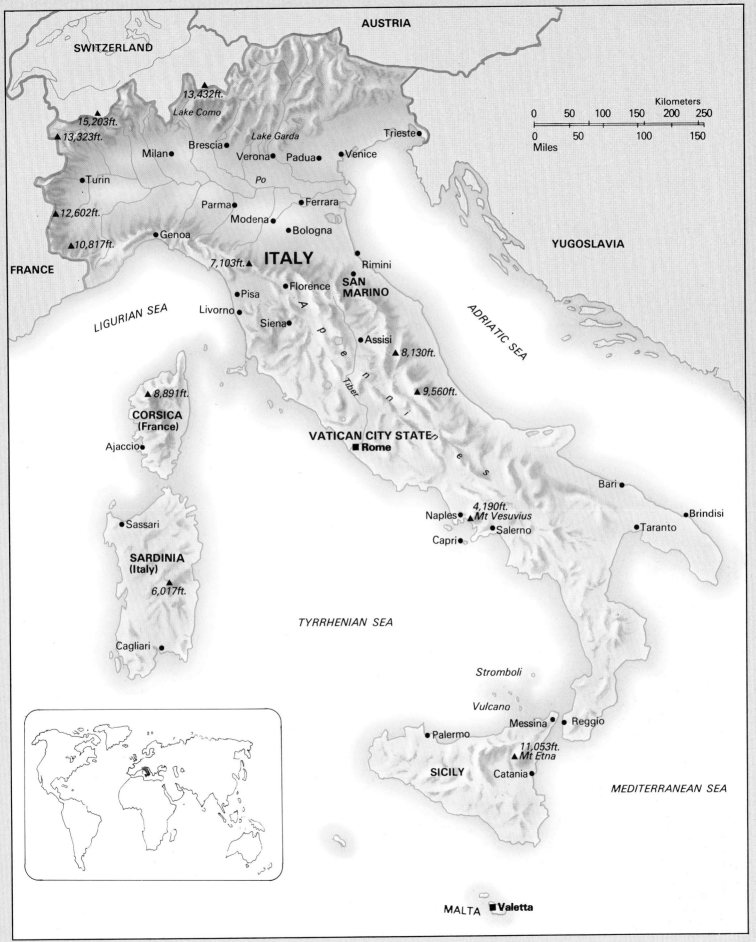

AUSTRIA

SWITZERLAND

▲ 13,432ft.

Lake Como

▲ 15,203ft.

▲ 13,323ft.

Lake Garda

Trieste ●

Milan ●

Brescia ●

Verona ●

Padua ●

Venice ●

Turin ●

Po

▲ 12,602ft.

Parma ●

Modena ●

Ferrara ●

Genoa ●

Bologna ●

▲ 10,817ft.

FRANCE

ITALY

7,103ft. ▲

Rimini ●

**SAN
MARINO**

YUGOSLAVIA

LIGURIAN SEA

Pisa ●

Florence ●

*A
p
e
n
n
i
n
e
s*

*ADRIATIC
SEA*

Livorno ●

Siena ●

Assisi ●

▲ 8,130ft.

Tiber

▲ 9,560ft.

▲ 8,891ft.

**CORSICA
(France)**

VATICAN CITY STATE
■ **Rome**

Ajaccio ●

Bari ●

Sassari ●

4,190ft.
Naples ● ▲ *Mt Vesuvius*

Brindisi ●

**SARDINIA
(Italy)**

Capri ●

Salerno ●

Taranto ●

▲
6,017ft.

Cagliari ●

TYRRHENIAN SEA

Stromboli

Vulcano

Messina ●

Reggio ●

Palermo ●

11,053ft.
▲ *Mt Etna*

SICILY

Catania ●

MEDITERRANEAN SEA

MALTA ■ **Valetta**

Kilometers
0   50   100   150   200   250
0   50   100   150
Miles

Poland, Czechoslovakia, and Hungary

Poland and Hungary are countries with vast areas of flat land. The fertile lowlands are good for farming and herds of cattle and horses graze on the wide open plains. Between these two countries lies Czechoslovakia. Here the snowcapped Carpathian Mountains tower over the land.

Poland is the largest country. It is a major world producer of coal. There are many big ports on the Baltic Sea where ships are built. Czechoslovakia and Hungary do not have any seaside but the river Danube links them with the sea. Barges carry goods along it to other countries in Europe.

Czechoslovakia, Poland, and Hungary have been *Communist* countries since 1945. In Communist countries, the government runs most factories and mines and many farms. Potatoes, wheat, and sugar beets are important crops on the farms. But since 1945 more and more Poles, Czechs, and Hungarians have been leaving their farms to work in mines and factories.

Poland

Czechoslovakia

Hungary

A view of Prague, capital of Czechoslovakia, in winter.

Above: Czechoslovakia is a country of mountains, basins, and valleys.
Right: Buda and Pest are shown with the river Danube in between. Together they make Budapest, the capital of Hungary.

Kilometers

0   50   100   150   200

0   50   100

Miles

BALTIC SEA

U S S R

Gdansk

Szczecin

Bydgoszcz

Netze

Vistula

Bug

Poznan

Warta

Warsaw

POLAND

Lodz

Oder

Lublin

Neisse

Wroclaw

Katowice

Krakow

Prague

Elbe

4,895ft.

Ostrava

Carpathian Mts

Plzen

CZECHOSLOVAKIA

Brno

8,711ft.

WEST
GERMANY

Vltava

Van

Kosice

Bratislava

Miskolc

AUSTRIA

Danube

Budapest

Debrecen

Tisza

Lake
Balaton

HUNGARY

ITALY

ROMANIA

Pecs

Szeged

YUGOSLAVIA

Workers harvest their crops on
a collective farm in Poland.

31

The Balkans and Romania

Bulgaria, Yugoslavia, Albania, and Greece make up the Balkan countries. Romania borders Bulgaria and Yugoslavia.

Greece consists of the mainland and over 1,400 islands. It is very mountainous and sheep and goats graze over the hills. Only one third of Greece is suitable for farming. But in spite of this, nearly half of the people live on the land. Many farmers grow grapes for making wine. Sometimes the grapes are picked, left to dry in the hot sun, then sold as raisins, currants, or sultanas.

Bulgaria, Yugoslavia, Albania, and Romania are also very mountainous. But, unlike Greece, the mountains are covered with forests where wolves, wild boars, and bears still live. Beneath the valuable forests there are rich deposits of copper, zinc, coal, and oil. Many people work in industry turning these minerals into useful products. Many others, especially in Albania, work on farms in the valleys.

Yugoslavia and Greece have beautiful beaches and islands. Thousands of people vacation there each year. Greece also has fascinating ruins from the times of the ancient Greeks.

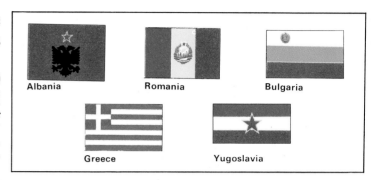

Albania   Romania   Bulgaria

Greece   Yugoslavia

Above: The Parthenon in Athens was built by the ancient Greeks.
Left: Many Romanians work on farms growing corn, wheat, and tobacco. They also raise sheep.
Below: Dubrovnik in Yugoslavia is well known for its beaches and medieval buildings.

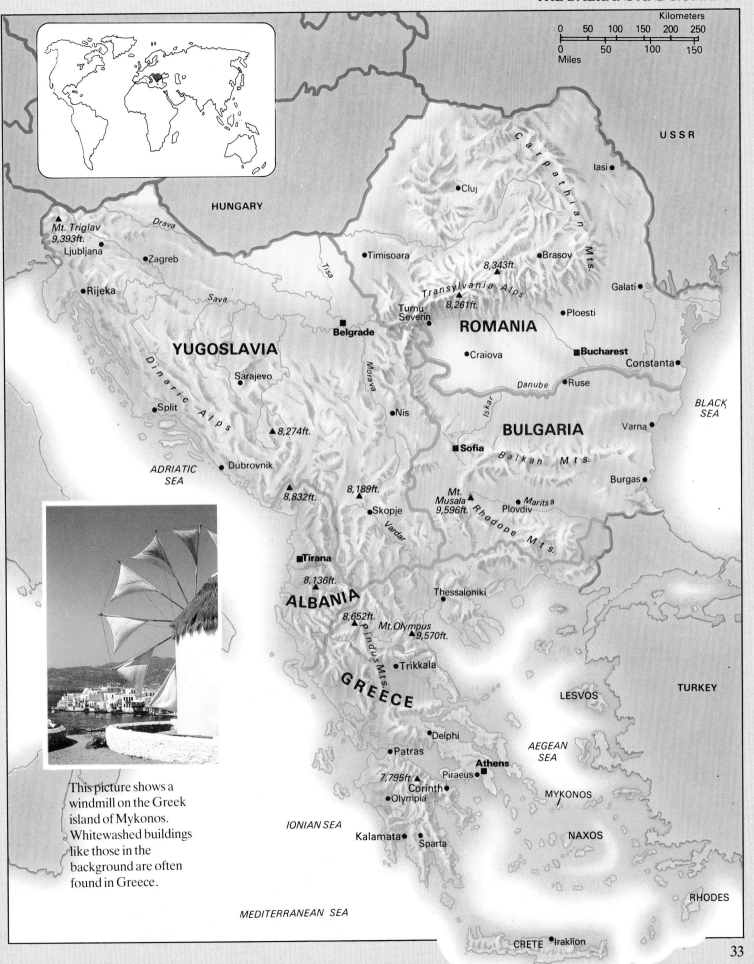

Kilometers

0 50 100 150 200 250

0 50 100 150

Miles

USSR

HUNGARY

▲ Mt. Triglav
9,393ft.

● Ljubljana

● Zagreb

Drava

Tisa

Sava

● Iasi

● Cluj

● Rijeka

Dinaric Alps

● Split

● Sarajevo

● Timisoara

8,343ft. ▲

Transylvania Alps

● Brasov

● Galati

8,261ft. ▲

Turnu
Severin ●

Belgrade ■

Morava

YUGOSLAVIA

ROMANIA

● Ploesti

● Craiova

Bucharest ■

▲ 8,274ft.

● Dubrovnik

*ADRIATIC
SEA*

Danube

● Ruse

● Nis

● Constanta

Iskar

Sofia ■

BULGARIA

Balkan Mts.

● Varna

*BLACK
SEA*

8,832ft. ▲

8,189ft. ▲

● Skopje

Vardar

● Burgas

Mt.
Musala ▲
9,596ft.

● Plovdiv

● Maritsa

Rhodope Mts.

Tirana ■

8,136ft. ▲

ALBANIA

● Thessaloniki

Pindus Mts.

8,652ft. ▲

Mt.Olympus ▲
9,570ft.

GREECE

● Trikkala

TURKEY

LESVOS

● Delphi

● Patras

*AEGEAN
SEA*

7,795ft. ▲

● Piraeus

Athens ■

● Corinth

MYKONOS

● Olympia

IONIAN SEA

NAXOS

● Kalamata

● Sparta

RHODES

MEDITERRANEAN SEA

CRETE ● Iraklion

This picture shows a
windmill on the Greek
island of Mykonos.
Whitewashed buildings
like those in the
background are often
found in Greece.

U.S.S.R.

The Union of Soviet Socialist Republics, the U.S.S.R., is the largest country in the world. It is more than twice the size of Canada, the second-largest country, and covers one sixth of the world's total land surface.

Since the Communist revolution in 1917, the U.S.S.R. has developed from an old-fashioned farming country into a powerful industrial nation. It has large *resources* of coal, oil, and natural gas. These provide fuel for the huge numbers of factories and industrial plants. The U.S.S.R., like the United States, has a large space industry. The first man and woman to be launched into space were Russians.

One fourth of the U.S.S.R. is farmland. Farmers work either on enormous state-owned farms or on smaller *collectives*. The U.S.S.R. is a leading producer of wheat, meat, and dairy products. It is divided into fifteen republics. These are made up of people of over a hundred groups—Ukranians, Uzbeks, Kazakhs, and many others. Over sixty languages are used in the U.S.S.R.. But Russian is spoken in most places because the Russian Federal Republic is the largest republic.

Left: Melons are sold at the market in Samarkand in the south of the U.S.S.R.

Right: On huge state farms in the Steppes wheat is harvested by combines. Most people live on farms and in cities west of the Ural Mountains. Farther east, over the mountains, there are high plains and vast forests. The Trans-Siberian Railway runs from Moscow in the west to Vladivostok in the east – over 5,600 miles.

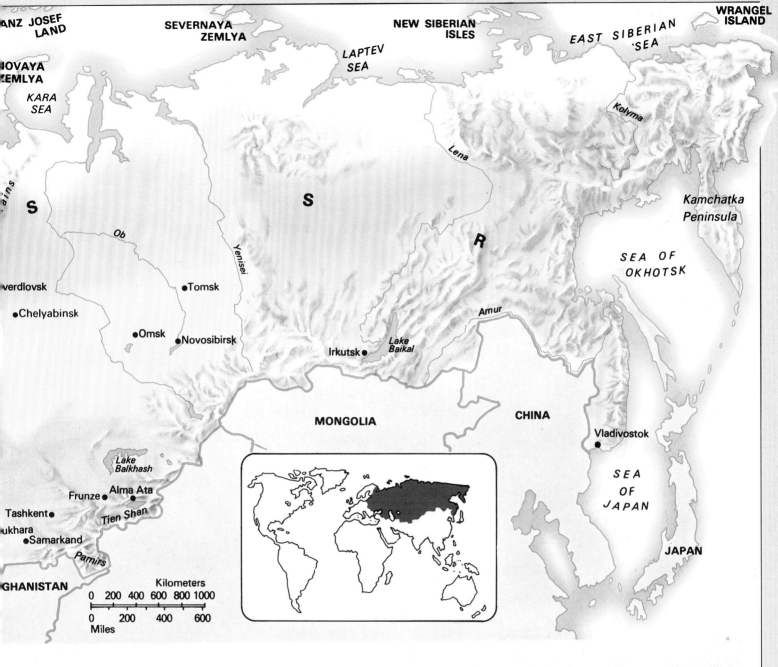

WRANGEL ISLAND

FRANZ JOSEF LAND

SEVERNAYA ZEMLYA

NEW SIBERIAN ISLES

EAST SIBERIAN SEA

NOVAYA ZEMLYA

LAPTEV SEA

KARA SEA

Kolyma

Lena

S

S

R

Kamchatka Peninsula

Ob

verdlovsk

Yenisei

•Chelyabinsk

•Tomsk

SEA OF OKHOTSK

•Omsk

•Novosibirsk

Amur

Irkutsk•

Lake Baikal

MONGOLIA

CHINA

Vladivostok

Lake Balkhash

Frunze •

Alma Ata •

SEA OF JAPAN

Tashkent•

Tien Shan

ukhara

•Samarkand

JAPAN

Pamirs

GHANISTAN

Kilometers

0 200 400 600 800 1000

0   200   400   600

Miles

Above: Inside the Kremlin (Russian for *fortress*) is the national museum. Lenin's tomb is in the foreground.
Left: Red Square and St. Basil's Cathedral in Moscow.

35

Southwest Asia

Most people living in the Middle East are Arabs. Their language is Arabic and their religion is Islam. Even in the non-Arab countries, Iran and Turkey, the people are Muslim. Many Christians live in Cyprus and Lebanon and most of the people in Israel are Jewish. The different religions of the people living in this area is the cause of constant trouble between them.

On the map you can see that most of this area is desert. Many of the people are farmers and the lack of rainfall is a serious problem.

On the Mediterranean coast, in river valleys and around *oases*, farms are irrigated with water from rivers and wells. But it is oil and not farming which has brought wealth to many countries in this area.

Every year pilgrims arrive in the Middle East. Jerusalem, the capital of Israel, is regarded as a holy city by Jews, Christians, and Muslims. Mecca and Medina in Saudi Arabia are Muslim holy cities.

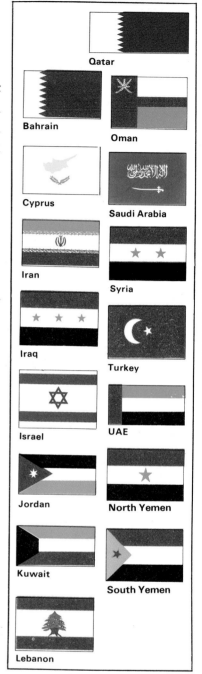

Qatar

Bahrain

Oman

Cyprus

Saudi Arabia

Iran

Syria

Iraq

Turkey

Israel

UAE

Jordan

North Yemen

Kuwait

South Yemen

Lebanon

Above: A road through the desert joins Abu Dhabi and Al Ain in the United Arab Emirates.

Below: Muslims make their pilgrimage to Mecca, birthplace of the prophet Muhammad.

Jews pray at the Wailing Wall in the Old City of Jerusalem. The Dome of the Rock, sacred to Muslims, is in the background.

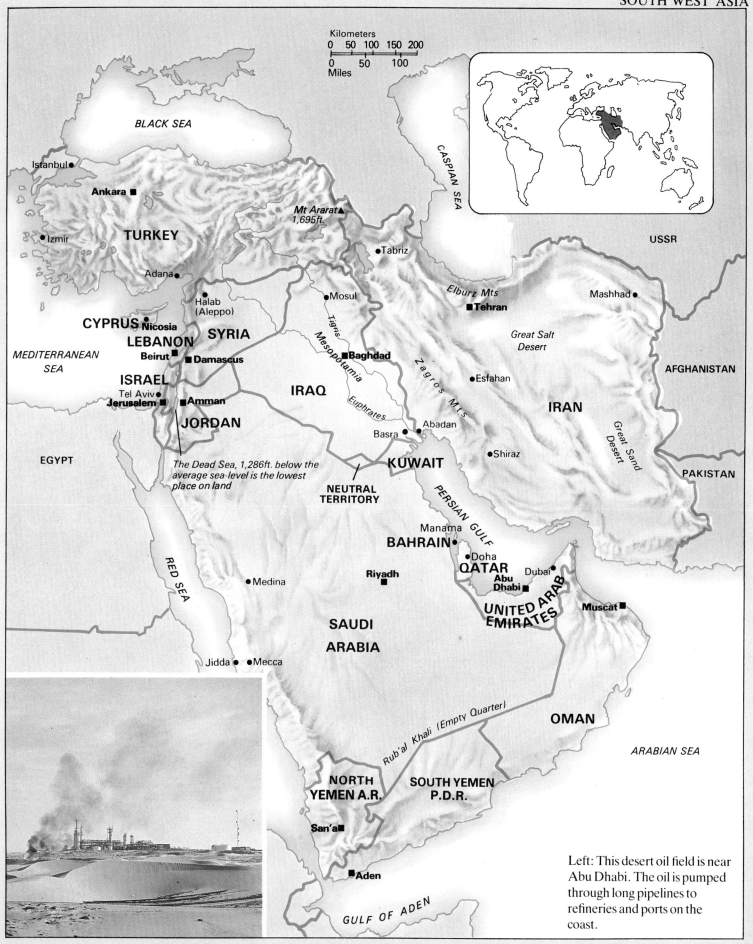

Kilometers
0 50 100 150 200
0 50 100
Miles

BLACK SEA

USSR

Istanbul

Ankara

Izmir

TURKEY

Adana

Mt Ararat
1,695ft.

Tabriz

CASPIAN SEA

Mashhad

Halab
(Aleppo)

Mosul

Elburz Mts

Tehran

CYPRUS Nicosia

LEBANON

SYRIA

Mesopotamia

Great Salt
Desert

AFGHANISTAN

MEDITERRANEAN
SEA

Beirut

Damascus

Tigris

Baghdad

Zagros Mts

Esfahan

IRAN

ISRAEL

Tel Aviv

IRAQ

Jerusalem

Amman

Euphrates

Abadan

Great Sand
Desert

JORDAN

Basra

Shiraz

PAKISTAN

EGYPT

The Dead Sea, 1,286ft. below the
average sea-level is the lowest
place on land

KUWAIT

NEUTRAL
TERRITORY

RED SEA

PERSIAN GULF

Manama

BAHRAIN

Doha

Dubai

Medina

Riyadh

QATAR

Abu
Dhabi

UNITED ARAB
EMIRATES

Muscat

SAUDI

ARABIA

Jidda

Mecca

Rub'al Khali (Empty Quarter)

OMAN

ARABIAN SEA

NORTH
YEMEN A.R.

SOUTH YEMEN
P.D.R.

Left: This desert oil field is near
Abu Dhabi. The oil is pumped
through long pipelines to
refineries and ports on the
coast.

San'a

Aden

GULF OF ADEN

India and Its Neighbors

This region contains the highest mountain range in the world—the Himalayas. It forms the boundary with Tibet and China and contains Mount Everest, the world's highest peak. On the map opposite you can trace the paths of three great rivers. They begin in the Himalayas and are the Ganges, the Indus, and the Brahmaputra.

India, Pakistan, and Bangladesh are thickly populated nations. Farming is the main occupation, but there is never enough food for the huge numbers of people. Many children start to work in the fields with their parents when they are very young. Farming methods are often very simple because there is little money for machinery or fertilizers. The *monsoon* climate is also a problem. It means that twice a year there are huge downpours of rain. If the rain is too heavy, it washes away crops. If the rains come too late, the crops may die. The Indian, Pakistani, and Bangladeshi governments are trying to set up more factories.

Religion is important in the everyday life of the people in this region. Most Indians are Hindu while most Pakistanis and Afghanis and many Bangladeshis are Muslim, followers of Islam.

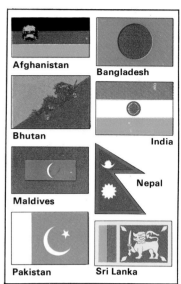

Afghanistan

Bangladesh

Bhutan

India

Maldives

Nepal

Pakistan

Sri Lanka

Above: Pilgrims bathe in the river Ganges at Varanasi, the Hindus' holy city.

Above right: The Taj Mahal is made of white marble. It is the tomb of a Mogul emperor and his favorite wife.

Right: This film poster is in New Delhi. More films are made in India than in any other country.

Far right: Women pick tea leaves in Darjeeling. Behind them is Mount Kanchenjunga.

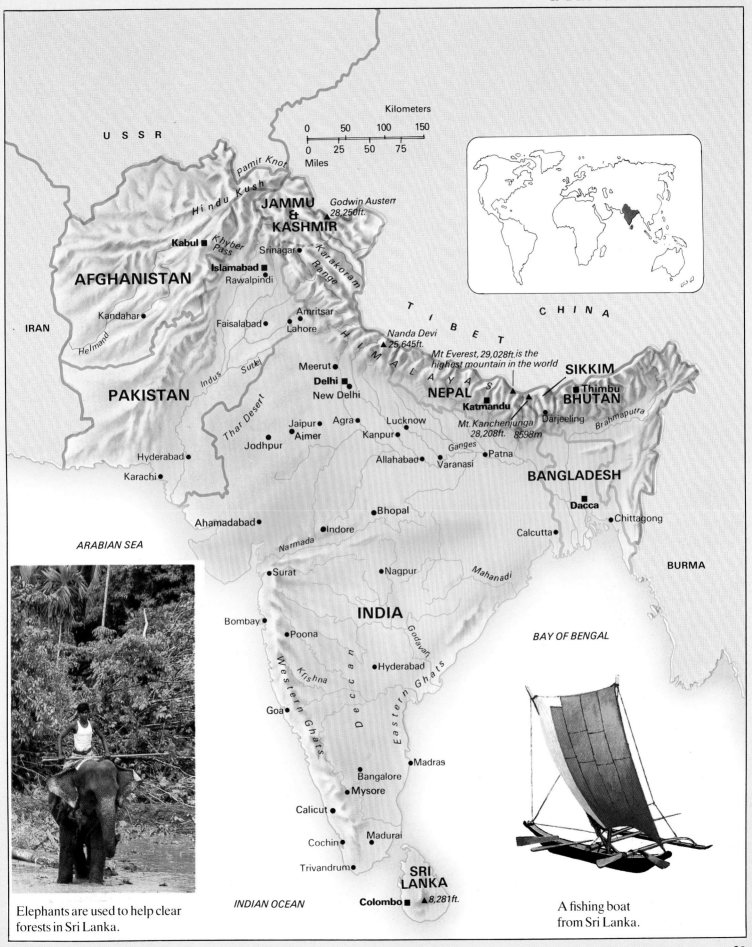

Kilometers

0 50 100 150

0 25 50 75
Miles

U S S R

Pamir Knot

Hindu Kush

JAMMU
&
KASHMIR

▲ Godwin Austen
28,250ft.

Kabul ■

Khyber Pass

Srinagar ●

AFGHANISTAN

Islamabad ■
Rawalpindi ●

IRAN

Kandahar ●

Helmand

PAKISTAN

Indus

Sutlej

Karakoram Range

Amritsar ●

Faisalabad ●
Lahore ●

T I B E T

C H I N A

H I M A L A Y A S

Nanda Devi
▲ 25,645ft.

Meerut ●

Delhi ■
New Delhi ●

Mt Everest, 29,028ft. is the highest mountain in the world

SIKKIM

NEPAL ▲ ▲

Thimbu ■
BHUTAN

Thar Desert

Jaipur ●
Ajmer ●

Agra ●

Lucknow ●

Katmandu ●

Mt. Kanchenjunga
28,208ft. 8598m

Darjeeling ●

Brahmaputra

Jodhpur ●

Kanpur ●

Ganges

Patna ●

Hyderabad ●

Allahabad ●
Varanasi ●

BANGLADESH

Karachi ●

Dacca ■

Ahamadabad ●

Narmada

Bhopal ●

Indore ●

Calcutta ●

Chittagong ●

ARABIAN SEA

Surat ●

Nagpur ●

Mahanadi

BURMA

INDIA

Godavari

BAY OF BENGAL

Bombay ●

Poona ●

Western Ghats

Krishna

Deccan

Eastern Ghats

Hyderabad ●

Goa ●

Madras ●

Bangalore ●
Mysore ●

Calicut ●

Madurai ●

Cochin ●

Trivandrum ●

SRI
LANKA

INDIAN OCEAN

Colombo ■ ▲ 8,281ft.

Elephants are used to help clear
forests in Sri Lanka.

A fishing boat
from Sri Lanka.

China

Nearly a fourth of all the people in the world live in China. It has more people than any other nation. Most people live in the fertile valleys of the Hwang Ho and Yangtze rivers and along the crowded coast. China is the third-largest country in the world. It stretches from the plateau of central Asia to the Pacific Ocean.

Since 1949 China has had a Communist government. Mao Zedong (Mao Tse-tung) was the leader of the government until his death in 1976. By encouraging everyone to put the needs of the community first, he helped turn China from a poor agricultural country into a great industrial one. Factories have been built all over China and many of the workers make iron and steel. But farming is still important and two thirds of the people are farmers.

Mongolia lies to the north of China. Most of the country is desert and the few people living there are wandering herdsmen. Many of them live in tents. On the map you can also see the peninsula of Korea. It is divided into two countries—North Korea and South Korea.

China

Mongolia

North Korea

South Korea

Above: The Great Wall of China is 1,490 miles long. It was built 2,500 years ago to keep Mongol invaders out.

Above right: A junk in Causeway Bay. Hong Kong has been a British colony for many years, but in 1997 it will return to China.

Right: Herdsmen in Mongolia lay the foundations for a tent, or *yurt*.

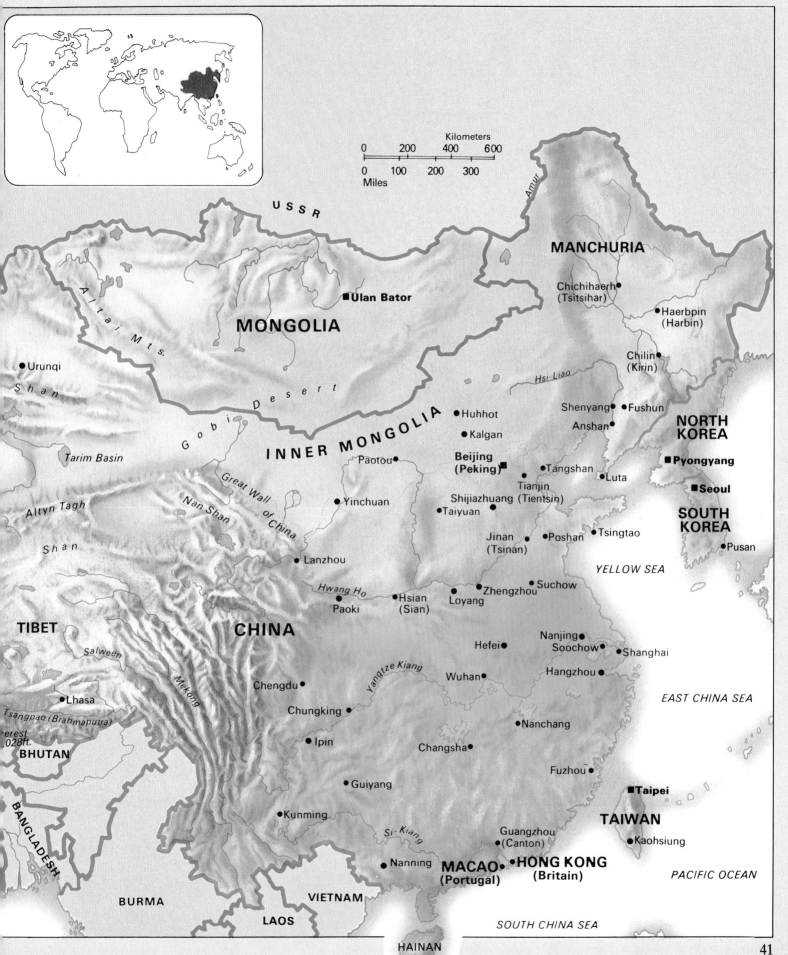

Kilometers

0   200   400   600

Miles

0   100   200   300

U S S R

MANCHURIA

Altai Mts.

■ Ulan Bator

MONGOLIA

Chichihaerh
(Tsitsihar)

• Haerbpin
(Harbin)

• Urunqi

Shan

Gobi Desert

Chilin
(Kirin)

Tarim Basin

INNER MONGOLIA

Hsi-Liao

Huhhot

Shenyang   • Fushun

NORTH
KOREA

Kalgan

Anshan

Altyn Tagh

Great Wall of China

Nan Shan

Paotou

Beijing
(Peking) ■

Tangshan

■ Pyongyang

Shan

Yinchuan

Tianjin
Shijiazhuang (Tientsin)
Taiyuan

Luta

■ Seoul

SOUTH
KOREA

Tsingtao

Lanzhou

Jinan
(Tsinan)

Poshan

• Pusan

TIBET

Salween

CHINA

Hwang Ho

Paoki

Hsian
(Sian)

Loyang

Zhengzhou

Suchow

YELLOW SEA

Lhasa

Mekong

Chengdu

Yangtze Kiang

Nanjing
Hefei   Soochow   Shanghai

Tsangpao (Brahmaputra)
erest
,028ft.

BHUTAN

Chungking

Wuhan

Hangzhou

EAST CHINA SEA

BANGLADESH

• Ipin

Changsha

Nanchang

Fuzhou

Guiyang

■ Taipei

Kunming

Si- Kiang

TAIWAN

Guangzhou
(Canton)

Kaohsiung

Nanning

MACAO
(Portugal)

HONG KONG
(Britain)

PACIFIC OCEAN

BURMA

VIETNAM

LAOS

SOUTH CHINA SEA

HAINAN

Japan

Japan consists of four main islands and about 3,000 smaller ones. From one end of the main islands to the other, there runs a volcanic mountain chain. Many of the volcanoes are still active. Mount Fuji, the highest peak, is a volcano, but it has not erupted since 1707. Earthquakes are common in Japan. There are over 1,000 each year, but most of them are only small tremors.

There is not much land suitable for farming in Japan because it is so mountainous. Rice is the main food crop on the little land which is cultivated. Fishing is important, for it provides food for the large population. Japanese cooks use shark fins and eels to make soup and seaweed is also a favorite dish.

Japan is the wealthiest country in Asia because it has an efficient manufacturing industry. Japanese workers make more cameras, television sets, and ships than any other country. There are many crowded industrial cities in Japan. But there are also peaceful temples and beautiful gardens.

Top: Television sets are checked on a conveyor belt in a Japanese factory. Other factories make cars, computers, watches, calculators, and stereos.

Above: Workers harvest rice in Japan. Rice grows well on flat land where there is heavy rainfall.

Left: The bullet train is also called the "Hikari Express." It is the world's fastest passenger train and it travels between Tokyo and Osaka. Mount Fuji is in the background.

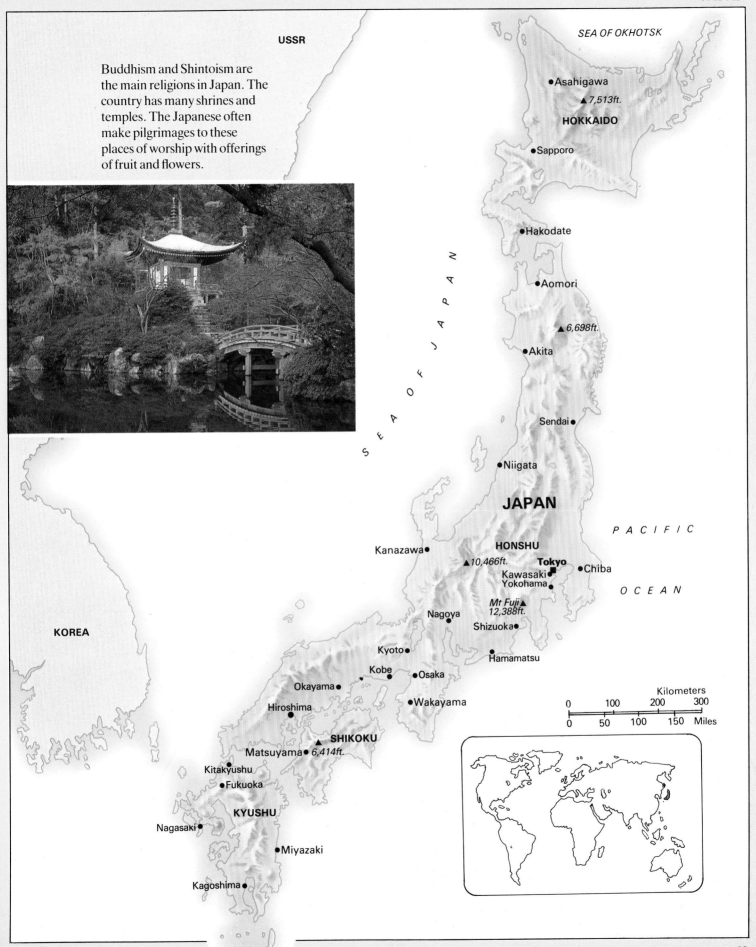

SEA OF OKHOTSK

USSR

Buddhism and Shintoism are the main religions in Japan. The country has many shrines and temples. The Japanese often make pilgrimages to these places of worship with offerings of fruit and flowers.

•Asahigawa

▲7,513ft.

HOKKAIDO

•Sapporo

•Hakodate

•Aomori

▲6,698ft.

•Akita

SEA OF JAPAN

•Sendai

•Niigata

JAPAN

HONSHU

Kanazawa•

▲10,466ft.

Tokyo

•Chiba

Kawasaki•

Yokohama•

PACIFIC

OCEAN

Mt Fuji▲

12,388ft.

Nagoya•

KOREA

Shizuoka•

Kyoto•

Hamamatsu•

Kobe•

•Osaka

Okayama•

•Wakayama

Hiroshima•

Kilometers

0   100   200   300

SHIKOKU

Matsuyama• 6,414ft.▲

0   50   100   150   Miles

Kitakyushu•

•Fukuoka

KYUSHU

Nagasaki•

•Miyazaki

Kagoshima•

Southeast Asia

Much of Southeast Asia is made up of volcanic islands. Indonesia has over 3,000 islands and the Philippines more than 7,000. All the countries have a similar hot, wet climate and much of the land is mountainous.

Southeast Asia is a heavily populated region. Many people live in stilt houses in fertile river valleys. Peasant farmers cut terraces into the hillsides where they grow rice, the main food crop. The slopes which are not tilled are covered in forest. There are also large rubber, coffee, and tobacco plantations in Indonesia, Malaysia, and Burma.

Mining is another important occupation in this region. Malaysia produces one third of the world's supply of tin. It is one of the richest countries in Southeast Asia. But many people in Vietnam and its neighboring countries are very poor because of years of war.

Music, dance, drama, and handmade crafts keep alive the ancient stories and legends of Southeast Asia. Islam and Buddhism are the main religions in this area.

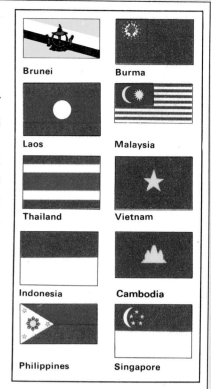

Brunei

Burma

Laos

Malaysia

Thailand

Vietnam

Indonesia

Cambodia

Philippines

Singapore

Left: Fruit and vegetables are paddled in from the countryside and sold at the floating market in Bangkok. The many canals in the city are called *klongs*.

Right: Rice grows in paddies on terraced hillsides in the Philippines. It has been grown this way for hundreds of years.

Below: Huge figures of demons guard a Buddhist temple in Bangkok.

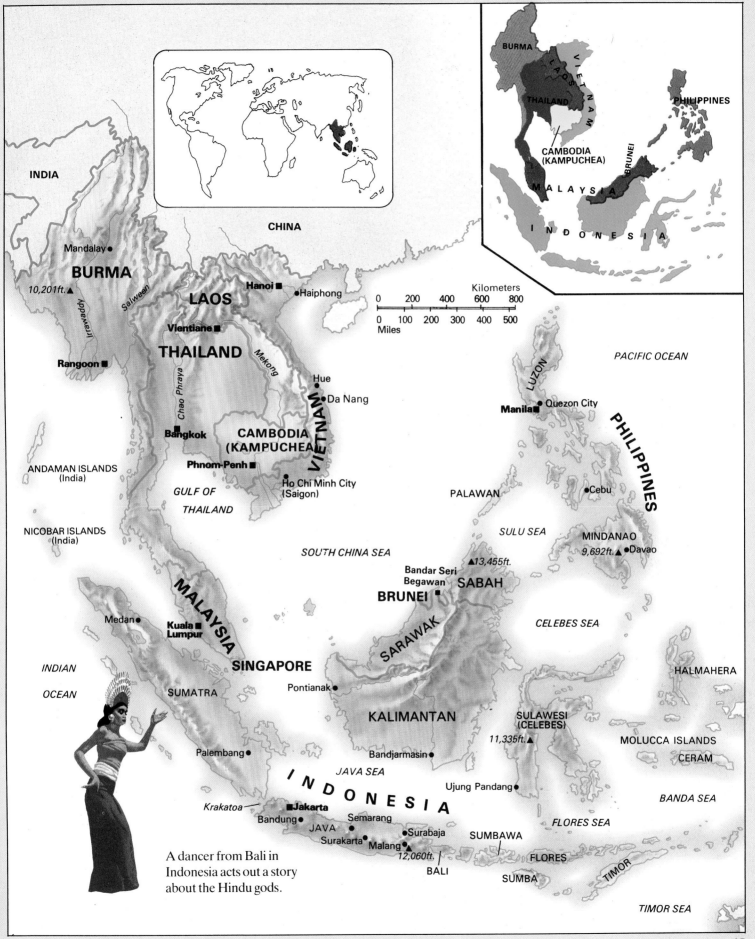

INDIA

CHINA

BURMA

Mandalay •

10,201ft. ▲

Salween

Irrawaddy

LAOS

Hanoi ■ • Haiphong

Vientiane ■

THAILAND

Mekong

Chao Phraya

Rangoon ■

Hue •
• Da Nang

VIETNAM

Bangkok ■

**CAMBODIA
(KAMPUCHEA)**

Phnom-Penh ■

Ho Chi Minh City
(Saigon) •

ANDAMAN ISLANDS
(India)

GULF OF
THAILAND

NICOBAR ISLANDS
(India)

SOUTH CHINA SEA

MALAYSIA

Medan •

**Kuala
Lumpur** ■

SINGAPORE

SUMATRA

INDIAN
OCEAN

Palembang •

Pontianak •

SARAWAK

KALIMANTAN

Bandjarmasin •

JAVA SEA

I N D O N E S I A

Krakatoa — **Jakarta** ■

Bandung •

JAVA

Semarang

Surakarta •

• Surabaja

Malang •

12,060ft. ▲

BALI

SUMBAWA

SUMBA

Kilometers
0 200 400 600 800

Miles
0 100 200 300 400 500

PACIFIC OCEAN

LUZON

Manila ■ • Quezon City

PHILIPPINES

PALAWAN

• Cebu

SULU SEA

MINDANAO
9,692ft. ▲ • Davao

▲13,455ft.

Bandar Seri
Begawan

SABAH

BRUNEI ■

CELEBES SEA

HALMAHERA

SULAWESI
(CELEBES)

11,335ft. ▲

MOLUCCA ISLANDS

CERAM

Ujung Pandang •

BANDA SEA

FLORES SEA

FLORES

TIMOR

TIMOR SEA

A dancer from Bali in
Indonesia acts out a story
about the Hindu gods.

Inset map:
BURMA
VIETNAM
LAOS
THAILAND
PHILIPPINES
CAMBODIA
(KAMPUCHEA)
BRUNEI
M A L A Y S I A
I N D O N E S I A

Canada

Canada is the second-largest country in the world. Only the U.S.S.R. is larger. Vast areas in the far north are uninhabited and only a small number of trappers and fishermen live in the snow-blanketed forests around the Hudson Bay.

Most Canadians live in the south, not far from the United States border, where the climate is warmer. The Prairie Provinces of Manitoba, Saskatchewan, and Alberta lie west of the Great Lakes. Sometimes they are called the "food basket of the world" because wheat farms stretch as far as the eye can see.

Canada's original people arrived there over 20,000 years ago. They came from Asia and their descendants today are the North American Indians and the Inuit (Eskimos). British and French settlers did not arrive until the seventeenth century.

Large deposits of minerals as well as fertile plains and rich forests help make Canada one of the wealthiest countries in the world. Canadians are proud too of their beautiful lakes and mountains and the cool, clean air of their forests.

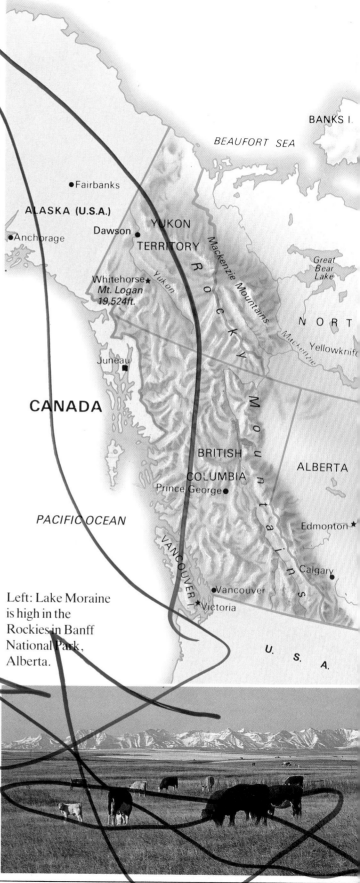

Left: Lake Moraine is high in the Rockies in Banff National Park, Alberta.

Top: Niagara Falls is on the border of Canada and the United States.
Above: Eskimo children build an igloo in Labrador.

QUEEN ELIZABETH ISLANDS

BAFFIN BAY

MELVILLE I.

DEVON I.

VICTORIA ISLAND

BAFFIN ISLAND

ATLANTIC OCEAN

WEST TERRITORIES

Slave Lake

HUDSON STRAIT

NEWFOUNDLAND

Lake Athabasca

HUDSON BAY

Churchill

Churchill

Nelson

LABRADOR

KATCHEWAN

MANITOBA

Saskatchewan

Saskatoon

Lake Winnipeg

QUEBEC

Albany

Fort Rupert

St John's ★

Regina ★

ONTARIO

PRINCE EDWARD I

Winnipeg ★

Kenora

Lake Nipigon

Charlottetown ★

Brandon

NEW BRUNSWICK

NOVA SCOTIA

Lake Superior

St Lawrence

Quebec ★

Fredericton ★

Halifax ★

Trois Rivieres

Sudbury

Montreal

Ottawa ■

Lake Michigan

Lake Huron

Left: Cattle graze on the foothills of the Rockies. East of the mountains, prairies and forests stretch all the way across the country to the Great Lakes.

Toronto ★

Lake Ontario

Hamilton

Niagara Falls

Lake Erie

Kilometers

0 200 400 600 800

0 100 200 300 400 500

Miles

★ = provincial capital

United States

The United States of America is the fourth-largest country in the world and has the fourth-largest population and land area. It is divided into fifty states and includes Alaska in the northwest and Hawaii, a group of islands in the Pacific Ocean.

Like Canada, the United States was first settled by Indians whose ancestors came from Asia. In the eighteenth and nineteenth centuries, large numbers of settlers came to the "New World" from Europe in search of a better way of life. These people first settled on the East Coast and started the first thirteen states. Blacks were brought over from Africa to work on the plantations. Gradually people with pioneering

Above: Yavapai Point, in Grand Canyon National Park, Arizona. The Canyon was formed by the Colorado River.

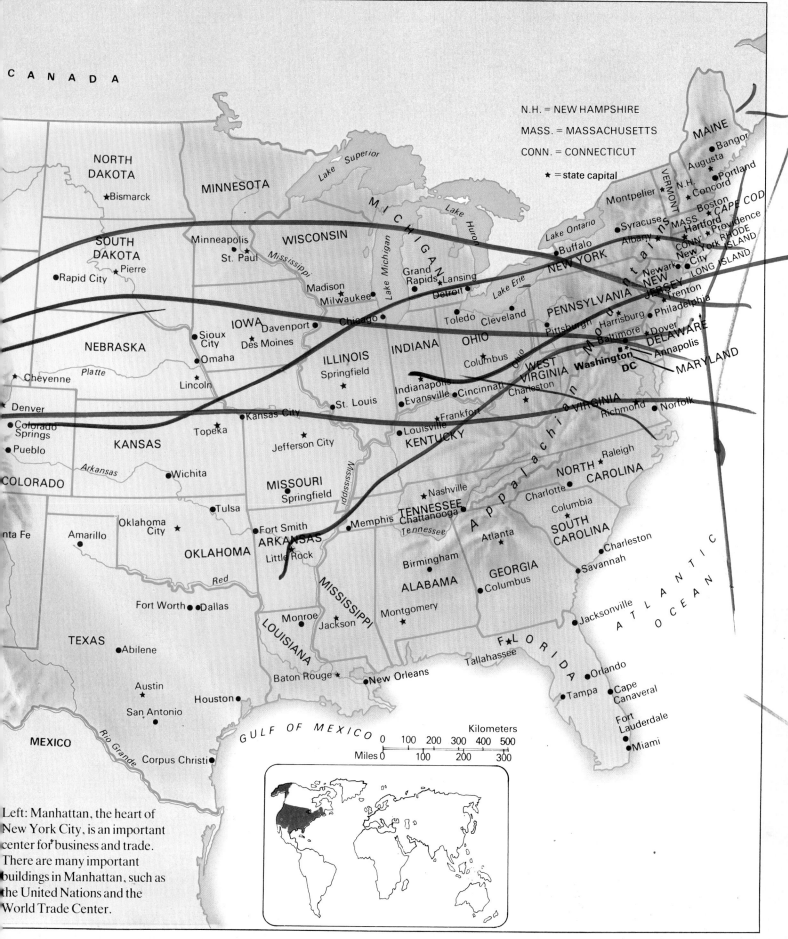

CANADA

N.H. = NEW HAMPSHIRE

MASS. = MASSACHUSETTS

CONN. = CONNECTICUT

★ = state capital

NORTH DAKOTA
★Bismarck

MINNESOTA

Lake Superior

MAINE
●Bangor
Augusta
Portland
Concord

VERMONT

N.H.

Montpelier

Lake Huron

Boston

CAPE COD

MICHIGAN

SOUTH DAKOTA
Minneapolis
●Rapid City ★Pierre
St. Paul

WISCONSIN

Mississippi

Lake Ontario

Syracuse

MASS.

Hartford

Providence

RHODE

Albany

CONN'

ISLAND

Buffalo

Newark

New York City

LONG ISLAND

Madison
★
Milwaukee

Grand Rapids

Lansing

Detroit

Lake Erie

NEW YORK

NEW JERSEY

Trenton

Lake Michigan

Chicago

Toledo

Cleveland

PENNSYLVANIA

Philadelphia

IOWA

Davenport

Pittsburgh

Harrisburg

Dover

DELAWARE

NEBRASKA

Sioux City

Des Moines

ILLINOIS

INDIANA

OHIO

Columbus

Ohio

Baltimore

Annapolis

Washington DC

MARYLAND

Omaha

Springfield

Indianapolis

Cincinnati

WEST VIRGINIA

★Cheyenne

Platte

Lincoln

St. Louis

Evansville

Charleston

VIRGINIA

Richmond

Norfolk

Denver

Kansas City

Frankfort

Colorado Springs

Topeka

Louisville

KENTUCKY

Pueblo

KANSAS

Jefferson City

Nashville

NORTH CAROLINA

Raleigh

COLORADO

Arkansas

Wichita

MISSOURI

Springfield

TENNESSEE

Chattanooga

Charlotte

Columbia

Appalachian

SOUTH CAROLINA

Tulsa

Tennessee

Memphis

Charleston

Oklahoma City ★

Fort Smith

Birmingham

Atlanta

Savannah

nta Fe

Amarillo

OKLAHOMA

ARKANSAS

Little Rock

GEORGIA

Columbus

ALABAMA

Red

MISSISSIPPI

Montgomery

Jacksonville

ATLANTIC OCEAN

Fort Worth ●Dallas

Monroe

Jackson

Tallahassee

FLORIDA

TEXAS ●Abilene

LOUISIANA

Baton Rouge ★New Orleans

Orlando

Austin

Houston

Cape Canaveral

San Antonio

GULF OF MEXICO

Fort Lauderdale

MEXICO

Rio Grande

Corpus Christi

Tampa

Miami

Kilometers

0 100 200 300 400 500

Miles 0   100   200   300

Left: Manhattan, the heart of New York City, is an important center for business and trade. There are many important buildings in Manhattan, such as the United Nations and the World Trade Center.

spirits ventured westward and new states were formed. Some farmed on the Midwestern plains while explorers and miners traveled through the Rocky Mountains to the Pacific coast. Today people from all over the world live in the United States.

Like their Canadian neighbors, most Americans have a high standard of living. The United States is an extremely wealthy country. It has large resources of oil, gas, coal, and many metals, huge farms and plantations and more factories than any other country in the world.

Above right: Las Vegas, Nevada, is famous for gambling and nightclubs.

Right: This view of the Delaware River shows the rich growth and beauty of the New Jersey region.

Left: Oil drilling is a common sight in Texas.

Below: The government of the United States includes the Senate and the House of Representatives. They meet in the Capitol building in Washington D.C.

Baseball is one of the most popular sports in the United States.

Eastern and Southern States

State	Popular name	Capital	Bird	Flower	Tree
Alabama	Yellowhammer State	Montgomery	Yellowhammer	Camellia	Southern pine (Longleaf pine)
Arkansas	Land of Opportunity	Little Rock	Mockingbird	Apple blossom	Pine
Connecticut	Constitution State	Hartford	Robin	Mountain laurel	White oak
Delaware	First State	Dover	Blue hen chicken	Peach blossom	American holly
Florida	Sunshine State	Tallahassee	Mockingbird	Orange blossom	Cabbage palm
Georgia	Empire State of the South	Atlanta	Brown thrasher	Cherokee rose	Live oak
Kentucky	Bluegrass State	Frankfort	Cardinal	Goldenrod	Tulip poplar
Louisiana	Pelican State	Baton Rouge	Brown pelican	Magnolia	Bald cypress
Maine	Pine Tree State	Augusta	Chickadee	White pine cone and tassel	White pine
Maryland	Old Line State	Annapolis	Baltimore oriole	Black-eyed Susan	White oak
Massachusetts	Bay State	Boston	Chickadee	Arbutus (Mayflower)	American elm
Mississippi	Magnolia State	Jackson	Mockingbird	Magnolia	Magnolia
New Hampshire	Granite State	Concord	Purple finch	Purple lilac	White birch
New Jersey	Garden State	Trenton	Eastern goldfinch	Purple violet	Red oak
New York	Empire State	Albany	Bluebird	Rose	Sugar maple
North Carolina	Tar Heel State	Raleigh	Cardinal	Flowering dogwood	Pine
Oklahoma	Sooner State	Oklahoma City	Scissor-tailed flycatcher	Mistletoe	Redbud
Pennsylvania	Keystone State	Harrisburg	Ruffed grouse	Mountain laurel	Hemlock
Rhode Island	Little Rhody	Providence	Rhode Island Red	Violet	Red maple
South Carolina	Palmetto State	Columbia	Carolina wren	Carolina jessamine	Palmetto
Tennessee	Volunteer State	Nashville	Mockingbird	Iris	Tulip poplar
Texas	Lone Star State	Austin	Mockingbird	Bluebonnet	Pecan
Vermont	Green Mountain State	Montpelier	Hermit thrush	Red clover	Sugar maple
Virginia	Old Dominion	Richmond	Cardinal	Flowering dogwood	none
West Virginia	Mountain State	Charleston	Cardinal	Rhododendron	Sugar maple

This small church among trees turning color is typical of the scenic Vermont countryside.

A New Orleans steamboat travels slowly along the Mississippi River.

N.H. = NEW HAMPSHIRE

MASS. = MASSACHUSETTS

CONN. = CONNECTICUT

The Midwest

State	Popular name	Capital	Bird	Flower	Tree
Illinois	Land of Lincoln	Springfield	Cardinal	Native violet	White oak
Indiana	Hoosier State	Indianapolis	Cardinal	Peony	Tulip tree or Yellow poplar
Iowa	Hawkeye State	Des Moines	Eastern goldfinch	Wild rose	Oak
Kansas	Sunflower State	Topeka	Western meadow lark	Sunflower	Cottonwood
Michigan	Wolverine State	Lansing	Robin	Apple blossom	White pine
Minnesota	Gopher State	St. Paul	Common loon	Pink and white lady's slipper	Norway or red pine
Missouri	Show Me State	Jefferson City	Bluebird	Hawthorn	Flowering dogwood
Nebraska	Cornhusker State	Lincoln	Western meadow lark	Goldenrod	American elm
North Dakota	Flickertail State	Bismarck	Western meadow lark	Wild prairie rose	American elm
Ohio	Buckeye State	Columbus	Cardinal	Scarlet carnation	Buckeye
South Dakota	Sunshine State	Pierre	Ring-necked pheasant	American pasque-flower	Black Hills spruce
Wisconsin	Badger State	Madison	Robin	Wood violet	Sugar maple

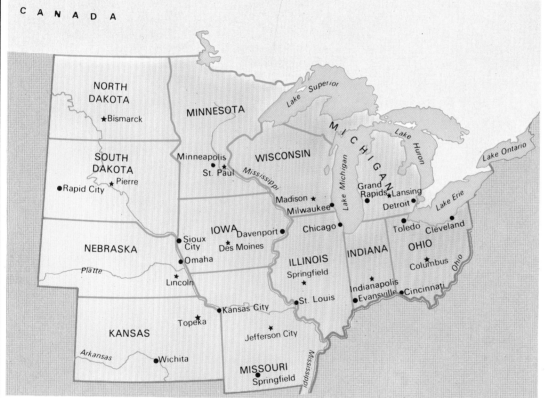

Automobile manufacturing is a very important industry in Detroit, Michigan. The industry provides jobs for many people. Car and truck parts are made and then they are assembled. This assembly line is at the Ford Motor Company.

Huge fields of soybeans have been planted on this farm in Iowa. Most of the midwest is covered by farmland. Other important crops are corn, wheat, tobacco, and maize. In addition, cattle, pigs, and sheep are often raised.

Western and Mountain States

State	Popular name	Capital	Bird	Flower	Tree
Alaska	Last Frontier	Juneau	Willow ptarmigan	Forget-me-not	Sitka spruce
Arizona	Grand Canyon State	Phoenix	Cactus wren	Saguaro	Paloverde
California	Golden State	Sacramento	California valley quail	Golden poppy	California redwood
Colorado	Centennial State	Denver	Lark bunting	Rocky Mt. columbine	Blue spruce
Hawaii	Aloha State	Honolulu	Nene (Hawaiian goose)	Hibiscus	Kukui
Idaho	Gem State	Boise	Mountain bluebird	Syringa (Mock orange)	Western white pine
Montana	Treasure State	Helena	Western meadow lark	Bitterroot	Ponderosa pine
Nevada	Silver State	Carson City	Mountain bluebird	Sagebrush	Single-leaf pinon
New Mexico	Land of Enchantment	Santa Fe	Road runner	Yucca	Pinon or nut pine
Oregon	Beaver State	Salem	Western meadow lark	Oregon grape	Douglas fir
Utah	Beehive State	Salt Lake City	Seagull	Sego lily	Blue spruce
Washington	Evergreen State	Olympia	Willow goldfinch	Coast rhododendron	Western hemlock
Wyoming	Equality State	Cheyenne	Meadow lark	Indian paintbrush	Cottonwood

Right: You can meet Mickey and Minnie Mouse and other Walt Disney characters in Disneyland. Disneyland is in California and Disneyworld is in Florida.

Cable cars run on tracks up and down the hilly streets of San Francisco.

For location of Alaska see (map) page 46; for Hawaii see (map) page 73.

Central America and

Antigua & Barbuda

Bahamas

Barbados

Cuba

Dominica

Dominican Republic

Grenada

St. Christopher Nevis

Haiti

Jamaica

St.Lucia

St.Vincent & Grenadines

Trinidad & Tobago

Mexico and seven small countries make up Central America—the land link between the United States and South America.

The people living in Central America and the islands of the West Indies are descendants either of the original people or of Europeans and blacks. Most of them speak Spanish, English, French, or American Indian languages. In 1492, when Christopher Columbus reached the islands in the Caribbean Sea, he thought he had sailed around the world to India. He called the people living there "Indians" and the islands were named the West Indies.

Central America and the thousands of West Indian islands are mostly hot and mountainous. The climate is ideal for growing fruit, coffee, cotton, tobacco, and sugarcane. Cuba is the largest of the West Indian islands and it is the third-largest producer of sugar in the world. Many of the islands are popular vacation places because of their sunny climate and easygoing atmosphere.

In Mexico most people work on small farms. The main crop is corn. A favorite meal is *tortillas*, a pancake made from corn flour. Gold and other metals are mined in Mexico, but the most important industry is oil.

Below left: The warm Caribbean Sea is ideal for sailing, swimming, and snorkeling.

the Caribbean

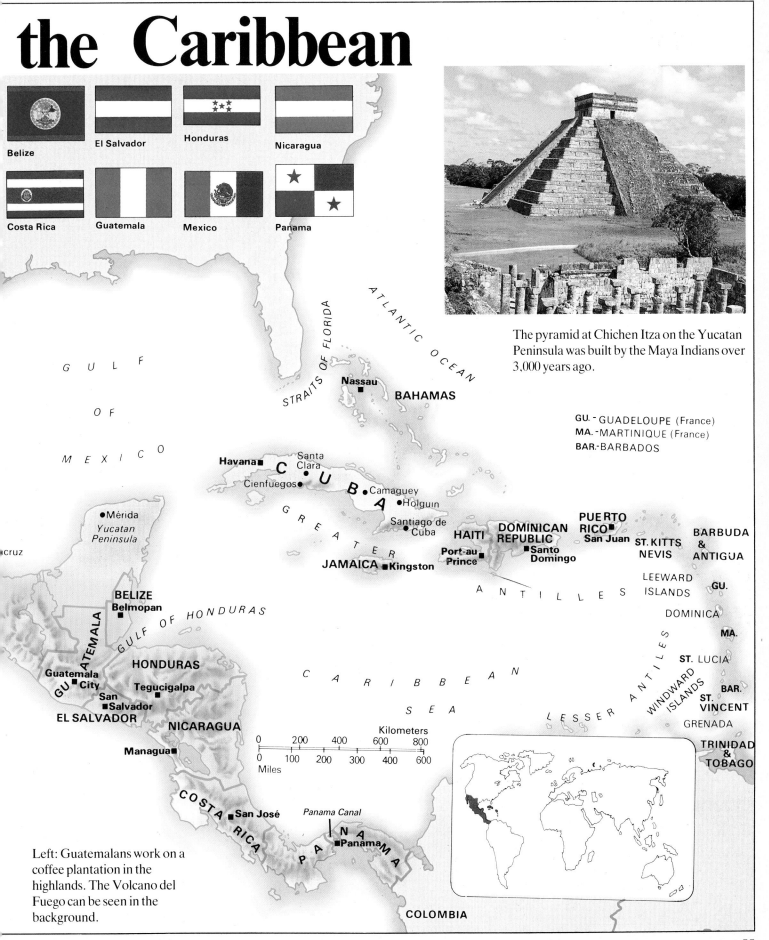

Belize

El Salvador

Honduras

Nicaragua

Costa Rica

Guatemala

Mexico

Panama

The pyramid at Chichen Itza on the Yucatan Peninsula was built by the Maya Indians over 3,000 years ago.

GU. - GUADELOUPE (France)
MA. - MARTINIQUE (France)
BAR. - BARBADOS

GULF

OF

MEXICO

STRAITS OF FLORIDA

ATLANTIC OCEAN

Nassau

BAHAMAS

Havana
Santa Clara
CUBA
Cienfuegos
Camaguey
Holguin
Santiago de Cuba

GREATER

ANTILLES

HAITI
Port-au-Prince

DOMINICAN REPUBLIC
Santo Domingo

PUERTO RICO
San Juan

ST. KITTS
NEVIS

BARBUDA & ANTIGUA

JAMAICA
Kingston

LEEWARD ISLANDS

GU.

DOMINICA

MA.

Mérida
Yucatan Peninsula

cruz

BELIZE
Belmopan

GULF OF HONDURAS

CARIBBEAN

SEA

LESSER ANTILLES

ST. LUCIA

WINDWARD ISLANDS

BAR.

ST. VINCENT

GRENADA

GUATEMALA
Guatemala City

HONDURAS

Tegucigalpa

San Salvador

EL SALVADOR

NICARAGUA

Managua

Kilometers
0 200 400 600 800
0 100 200 300 400 600
Miles

TRINIDAD & TOBAGO

COSTA RICA
San José

Panama Canal

PANAMA
Panama

Left: Guatemalans work on a coffee plantation in the highlands. The Volcano del Fuego can be seen in the background.

COLOMBIA

55

The Andean Countries

The Andes Mountains rise above much of Colombia, Ecuador, Peru, and Bolivia. They form high tablelands, or *plateaus*, where the climate is cool even though the equator passes through Ecuador and Colombia. Many rivers that feed the Amazon River begin in the Andes and travel eastward through thick tropical forests.

Bananas and coffee are grown on plantations where the climate is hot and tropical. As transport across the mountains gets better, more people are living in the Amazon lowlands. Here they farm and work in mines. But much of the land is covered by thick forest and cannot be farmed.

Over 800 years ago the Andes were populated by the Incas. Gold and silver in the mountains attracted the Spaniards, who eventually destroyed the Inca civilization. Today minerals are still important, especially in Bolivia. Spanish is the official language spoken in the Andean countries.

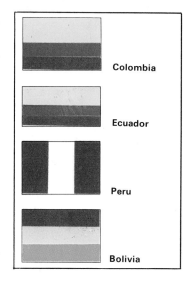

Colombia

Ecuador

Peru

Bolivia

Left: Llamas are herded in the Andes near Cuzco, Peru. Their wool is used to make warm clothing.

Below: Indians live in the interior of Colombia, far from the modern world. In this picture rice is pounded with a large mortar and pestles.

Above: Indians in colorful clothes gather in a market in Ecuador to sell their fruit and vegetables. Many Indians in the Andean countries still speak the old Indian languages: Quechua and Aymara.

Below: Traditional reed boats lie on the beaches of Lake Titicaca in Peru. Some Peruvians make their living by fishing in the lake and farming the surrounding land.

PANAMA

Cartagena●
●Barranquilla
19,029ft.▲

Medellin●
●Bucaramanga
VENEZUELA
GUYANA

Magdalena
■Bogotá

Cali●
COLOMBIA
18,865ft.▲

20,561ft.■Quito
Guayaquil●
ECUADOR
Amazon

Iquitos●
BRAZIL

Piura●
Marañon
Andes

Chiclayo●
Trujillo●
Chimbote●
22,205ft.▲

Madeira

PERU

Callao●
■Lima
●Huancayo
Beni

Cuzco●
20,945ft.▲
El Misti
19,101ft.▲
Lake
Titicaca
Arequipa●
Lake
Titicaca
BOLIVIA
■La Paz
Cochabamba●
●Santa Cruz

Lake
Poopo
■Sucre

22,162ft.▲

CHILE
PARAGUAY

PACIFIC

OCEAN

22,572ft.

ARGENTINA

22,831ft.

Mountains

Kilometers
0   200   400   600   800
0   100 200 300 400 500
Miles

57

Brazil and Its Neighbors

People of many different races live together in eastern South America. There are American Indians and *mestizos*, who are mixed Indian and European people. Other people are direct descendants of Europeans or Africans. Most of the early settlers were Spanish or Portuguese and most South Americans today speak one of these languages. Many people are also Roman Catholic.

Brazil is the largest country in South America. Much of the land is covered in thick Amazon rain forest. Most people live in big cities, such as Rio de Janeiro and Sao Paulo near the Atlantic coast. The northeastern part of Brazil is poorer. Land is owned by a few rich landlords who employ farmers. In bad years the farmers have to go to the cities in search of other work.

Brazil is famous for growing coffee. Sugar cane is also an important crop. Coal, iron ore, and other minerals are abundant in Brazil.

To the northeast of Brazil is Venezuela. Here rain forests also cover much of the land. Venezuela is a very rich country because it has valuable oil fields and iron ore. The money received from selling oil provides Venezuelans with factories, modern homes, and roads.

Guyana, Surinam, and French Guiana were once colonies of the British, Dutch, and French. In these countries most people live in cities along the coast.

Above: The Amazon River flows through the thick, hot jungle. It is part of the world's greatest river system.

Left: The Indians living in the Mato Grosso region of Brazil often wear traditional face paint.

Right: A huge statue of Christ watches over Corcovado Peak and the beautiful harbor of Rio de Janeiro. A lively carnival takes place in this city every year.

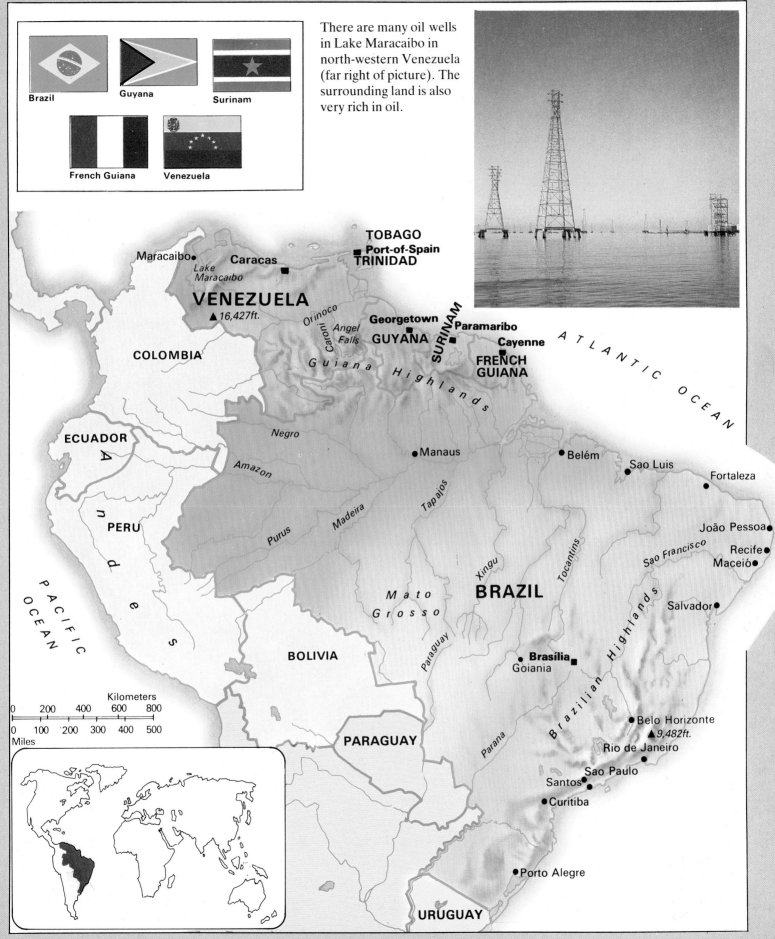

Brazil

Guyana

Surinam

French Guiana

Venezuela

There are many oil wells in Lake Maracaibo in north-western Venezuela (far right of picture). The surrounding land is also very rich in oil.

Maracaibo

Caracas

TOBAGO
Port-of-Spain
TRINIDAD

Lake Maracaibo

VENEZUELA
▲ 16,427ft.

COLOMBIA

Orinoco

Caroni

Angel Falls

Georgetown
GUYANA

Paramaribo
SURINAM

Cayenne
FRENCH GUIANA

ATLANTIC OCEAN

Guiana Highlands

ECUADOR

Negro

Amazon

Manaus

Belém

Sao Luis

Fortaleza

A n d e s

PERU

Purus

Madeira

Tapajos

João Pessoa

Sao Francisco

Recife
Maceió

PACIFIC OCEAN

Xingu

Mato Grosso

Tocantins

BRAZIL

Salvador

BOLIVIA

Paraguay

Brasília
Goiania

Brazilian Highlands

Kilometers
0 200 400 600 800
0 100 200 300 400 500
Miles

Parana

Belo Horizonte
▲ 9,482ft.

Rio de Janeiro

Sao Paulo

Santos

Curitiba

PARAGUAY

Porto Alegre

URUGUAY

Southern South America

The countries of southern South America enjoy a mild climate, unlike their neighbors in the tropical north. The southern tip of the continent is very cool because it is not far from the frozen wastes of Antarctica.

Chile is long and narrow. In the north is the Atacama Desert, where workers mine copper and nitrate. Many people in Chile try to live off the land, but farming is hard in most areas. People are leaving their farms to work in cities such as Santiago and Valparaiso.

Argentina is the second-largest and the richest of all South American countries. Farmers rear sheep and cattle and grow wheat, sugar cane, and cotton on the fertile *pampas*, or grasslands. Factory workers in the cities process these products.

Most people living in Chile and Argentina are descendants of the Spanish and are Spanish-speaking. People from Europe, especially from Italy, still live in these countries today.

Argentina

Chile

Paraguay

Uruguay

Above: Patagonia is the name of the upland plain in the south of Argentina. There are oil, coal, and mineral deposits in this region.

Above left: Buenos Aires is the major port of Argentina.

Left: The copper mine at Chiquicamata in Chile is the largest open cast mine in the world.

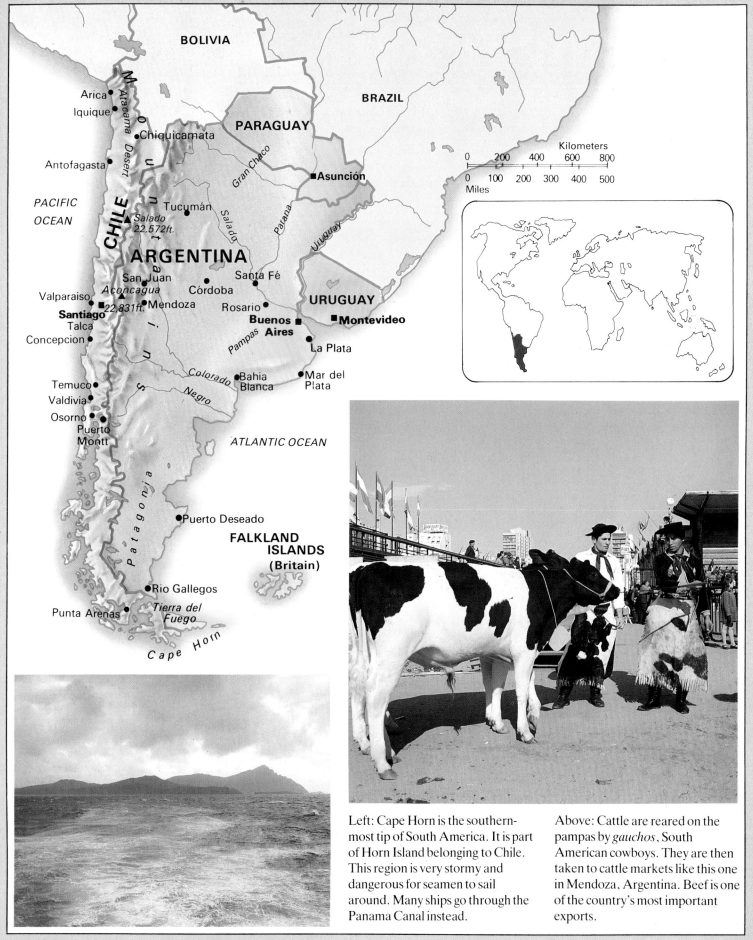

BOLIVIA

BRAZIL

PARAGUAY

Arica
Iquique
Chiquicamata
Antofagasta

Atacama Desert

Gran Chaco

■ Asunción

PACIFIC
OCEAN

CHILE

Tucumán

Salado
22,572ft.

ARGENTINA

San Juan
Aconcagua
Valparaiso
22,831ft.
Santiago
Talca
Concepcion

Córdoba
Mendoza
Rosario
Buenos
Aires
La Plata

Santa Fé

URUGUAY

■ Montevideo

Pampas

Temuco
Valdivia
Osorno
Puerto
Montt

Colorado

Bahia
Blanca

Mar del
Plata

Negro

ATLANTIC OCEAN

Patagonia

Puerto Deseado

FALKLAND
ISLANDS
(Britain)

Rio Gallegos

Punta Arenas

Tierra del
Fuego

Cape Horn

Kilometers
0 200 400 600 800
0 100 200 300 400 500
Miles

Left: Cape Horn is the southern-
most tip of South America. It is part
of Horn Island belonging to Chile.
This region is very stormy and
dangerous for seamen to sail
around. Many ships go through the
Panama Canal instead.

Above: Cattle are reared on the
pampas by *gauchos*, South
American cowboys. They are then
taken to cattle markets like this one
in Mendoza, Argentina. Beef is one
of the country's most important
exports.

North Africa

The vast Sahara Desert covers almost all of northern Africa. It is the largest, hottest desert in the world, stretching for 3,000 miles from the Atlantic Ocean to the Red Sea. In the northwest, in Morocco and Algeria, lie the rugged Atlas Mountains.

The people of northern Africa are mostly Muslim Arabs and Berbers who earn their living from farming. They live in river valleys and around oases because there is no water in other areas. In Egypt it scarcely ever rains, except along the Mediterranean coast. Most farmers rely on the river Nile for water. The Aswan Dam, built on the Nile, stores water for use during dry periods.

Tourists travel to Tunisia and Morocco to enjoy sunbathing on the beaches and wandering through the colorful bazaars. But many more tourists visit Egypt to see the pyramids at Giza—one of the Seven Wonders of the World.

Below: The pyramids at Giza were built to be the burial tombs for the kings of Ancient Egypt.
Below right: In Mali boats carry goods along the Niger River.
Far right: Flare stacks around a desert oil field in Libya.

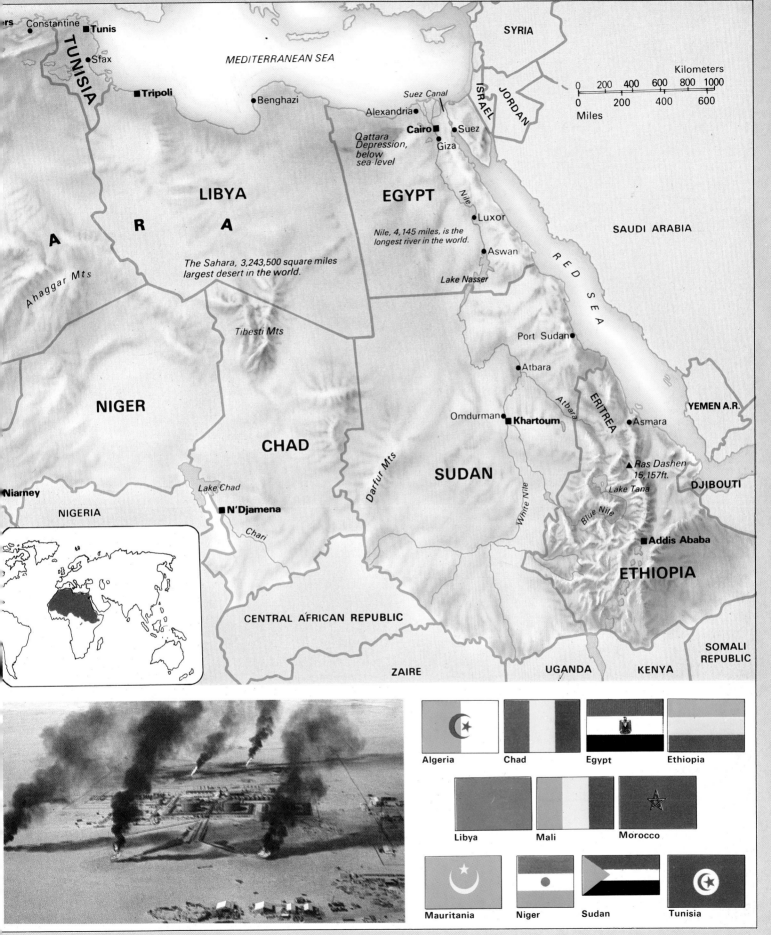

rs
Constantine • ■ Tunis
TUNISIA
• Sfax

MEDITERRANEAN SEA

■ Tripoli
• Benghazi

SYRIA
ISRAEL
JORDAN

Kilometers
0 200 400 600 800 1000
0   200   400   600
Miles

Suez Canal
Alexandria •
Cairo ■ ■ • Suez
Giza •

Qattara
Depression,
below
sea-level

LIBYA

S A

R A

A

Ahaggar Mts

The Sahara, 3,243,500 square miles
largest desert in the world.

Tibesti Mts

EGYPT

Nile

• Luxor

Nile, 4,145 miles, is the
longest river in the world.

• Aswan

Lake Nasser

SAUDI ARABIA

R E D   S E A

NIGER

CHAD

Lake Chad

Darfur Mts

Port Sudan •

Atbara •

Atbara

Omdurman • ■ **Khartoum**

SUDAN

White Nile

ERITREA

• Asmara

YEMEN A.R.

▲ Ras Dashen
15,157ft.

Lake Tana

Blue Nile

DJIBOUTI

Niarney

NIGERIA

■ N'Djamena

Chari

■ **Addis Ababa**

ETHIOPIA

CENTRAL AFRICAN REPUBLIC

ZAIRE   UGANDA   KENYA

SOMALI
REPUBLIC

Algeria   Chad   Egypt   Ethiopia

Libya   Mali   Morocco

Mauritania   Niger   Sudan   Tunisia

West Africa

West Africa is a jigsaw puzzle of countries. Many different groups of black Africans live there. Nigeria alone has 250 groups. The people speak a number of African languages, including Swahili. But official languages are often English, French, or Portuguese because most of these countries were once ruled by these European nations.

The countries along the coast are hot and have long, wet seasons. They are largely covered by tropical forest. Cocoa, coffee, palm oil, and rubber are important crops. Root crops of cassava and yams provide food. Farther inland, on savanna grasslands, crops consist of cotton and groundnuts. Millet, corn, and sorghum are grown for food. Cattle are kept for their meat, as well as for their hides and skins.

West African countries are building up their industries. There are new factories in Nigeria and Senegal, metals are mined in Sierra Leone and Ghana, and oil is drilled in Nigeria.

Crops and minerals are exported and the money received from selling these products is used to build modern towns, schools, and hospitals. But many of the people still live on the land in the same way as their families have lived for centuries. Some live in clearings in the hot forests and work small gardens. Others herd animals on the *savanna* grasslands.

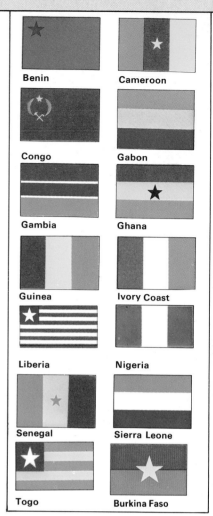

Benin   Cameroon

Congo   Gabon

Gambia   Ghana

Guinea   Ivory Coast

Liberia   Nigeria

Senegal   Sierra Leone

Togo   Burkina Faso

Left: A Nigerian woman in colorful dress stands in the center of Lagos, the modern capital of Nigeria.

Below: Cocoa trees grow on large plantations in Ghana. Their huge pods are cut off with large knives. The beans inside are then dried and used to make chocolate and cocoa.

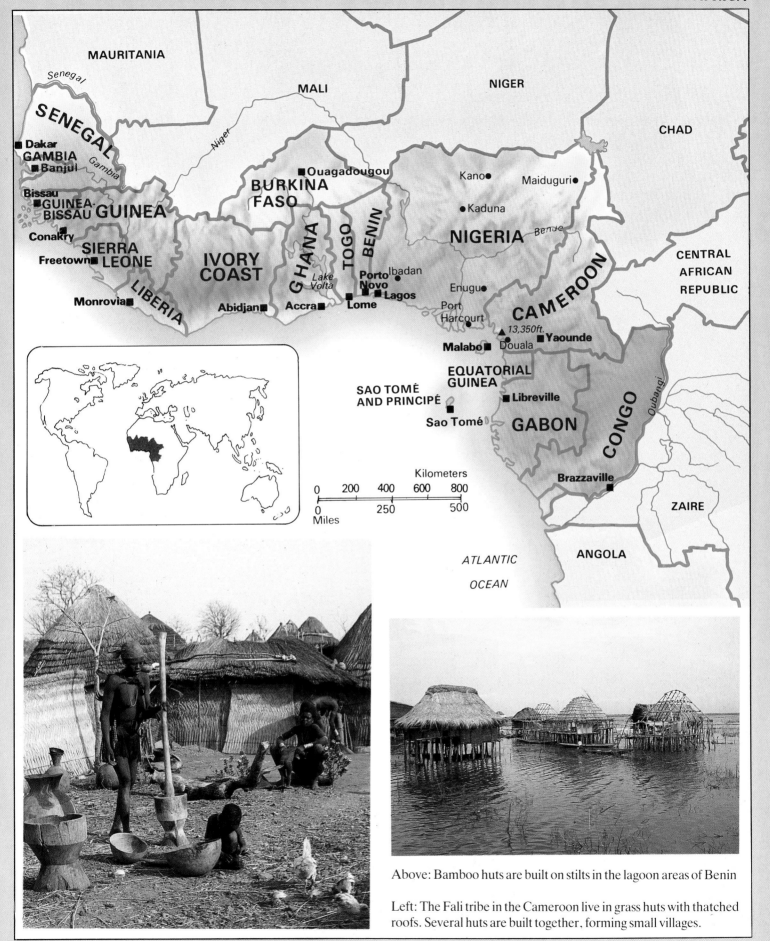

MAURITANIA

Senegal

SENEGAL

MALI

NIGER

CHAD

■ Dakar
GAMBIA
■ Banjul

Niger

Gambia

Bissau
■ GUINEA-
BISSAU GUINEA

BURKINA
FASO

● Ouagadougou

Kano ●

Maiduguri ●

● Kaduna

NIGERIA

Benue

CENTRAL
AFRICAN
REPUBLIC

Conakry ■

SIERRA
LEONE
Freetown ■

IVORY
COAST

G
H
A
N
A

T
O
G
O

B
E
N
I
N

Ibadan ●

Enugu ●

CAMEROON

Monrovia ■

LIBERIA

Abidjan ■

Accra ■

Lake
Volta

Porto
Novo ●
● Lagos
Lome ■

Port
Harcourt ●

▲ 13,350ft.
● Yaounde
Douala

EQUATORIAL
GUINEA

Malabo ■

SAO TOMÉ
AND PRINCIPÉ

● Libreville

GABON

C
O
N
G
O

Oubangi

Sao Tomé ●

Kilometers

0   200   400   600   800

0   250   500
Miles

Brazzaville ■

ZAIRE

ATLANTIC

OCEAN

ANGOLA

Above: Bamboo huts are built on stilts in the lagoon areas of Benin

Left: The Fali tribe in the Cameroon live in grass huts with thatched roofs. Several huts are built together, forming small villages.

65

Central and East Africa

Much of Central Africa is lowland covered with thick tropical forest. One of the greatest rivers in Africa, the river Zaire, runs through the region and is important for transport. Most people in Central Africa live in small clearings, growing food crops such as yams and cassava. Sometimes parts of the forest are cleared for timber. Cocoa, coffee, palm oil, and rubber are also important. Zaire's main source of wealth comes from copper mines in the southeastern part of the country.

East Africa is a region of highland and *savanna* grassland. A cool climate is typical of the East African plateau. In the past Europeans settled in this area, growing tea, coffee, cotton, and sisal. Food crops consist of millet, corn, and plantains.

Tourists often travel to Kenya to see wild animals. Once hunted, many lions, elephants, zebras, and rhinos now live on large game reserves.

Somalia and Djibouti are mostly desert. The people living in these countries are animal herders and are often very poor.

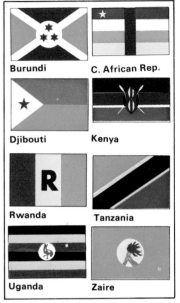

Burundi   C. African Rep.

Djibouti   Kenya

Rwanda   Tanzania

Uganda   Zaire

The Bambuti, a tribe of pygmies, live in the forests of Zaire. They are the world's smallest people. They hunt game with spears, bows and arrows, and fish with nets.

An elephant herd grazes on the grasslands of Kenya. Behind them is Mount Kilimanjaro, the highest peak in Africa.

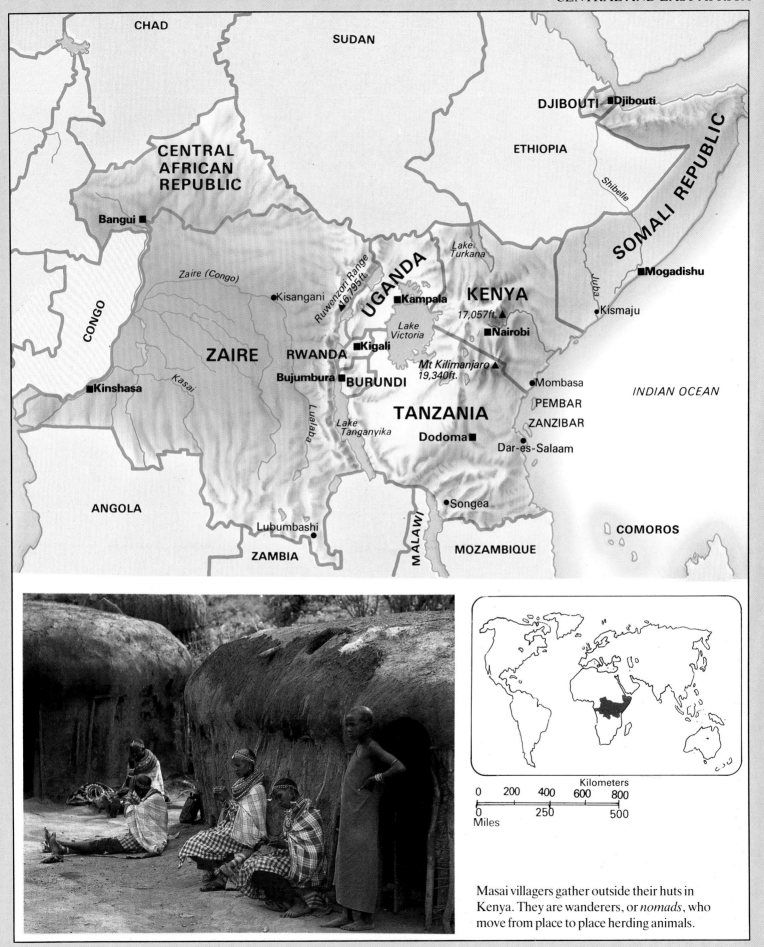

CHAD

SUDAN

DJIBOUTI ■Djibouti

ETHIOPIA

CENTRAL
AFRICAN
REPUBLIC

SOMALI REPUBLIC

Shibelle

Bangui ■

Zaire (Congo)

Lake
Turkana

■Mogadishu

Kisangani ●

Ruwenzori Range
▲16,795ft.

UGANDA
■Kampala

KENYA

17,057ft.▲

Juba

● Kismaju

CONGO

Lake
Victoria

■Nairobi

ZAIRE

RWANDA

■Kigali

Mt Kilimanjaro ▲
19,340ft.

● Mombasa

INDIAN OCEAN

Kasai

Bujumbura ■
■BURUNDI

PEMBAR

■ Kinshasa

TANZANIA

ZANZIBAR

Lualaba

Lake
Tanganyika

Dodoma ■

Dar-es-Salaam ●

ANGOLA

● Songea

COMOROS

Lubumbashi ●

ZAMBIA

MALAWI

MOZAMBIQUE

Kilometers
0   200   400   600   800

0   250   500
Miles

Masai villagers gather outside their huts in
Kenya. They are wanderers, or *nomads*, who
move from place to place herding animals.

Southern Africa

Southern Africa is very different from the rest of Africa. To start with, its climate is cooler than the rest of Africa. Look for the Namib and Kalahari deserts on the map. Unlike the almost barren Sahara in northern Africa, the Kalahari is a dry, bush-covered plateau.

Many Europeans also live in this part of Africa. Large numbers of them first arrived in South Africa during the 1880s, attracted by the discovery of gold. Many stayed to farm the land or run mines and businesses.

South Africa and Zimbabwe are the richest countries in southern Africa. People from poorer countries, such as Botswana and Lesotho, often go to work in their large manufacturing industries. South Africa produces a huge share of the world's gold and diamonds. In Zimbabwe there are large cattle ranches as well as corn, cotton, and tobacco farms.

In South Africa there is a government policy called *apartheid* to keep Europeans and black Africans apart. Europeans control the government and own the major businesses. Madagascar is one of the largest islands in the world. Most people are farmers.

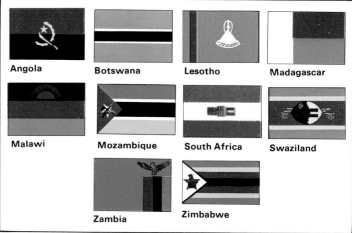

Angola   Botswana   Lesotho   Madagascar

Malawi   Mozambique   South Africa   Swaziland

Zambia   Zimbabwe

Above: Lake Kariba is on the border of Zimbabwe and Zambia. The Kariba Dam in Zimbabwe provides water for the dry season.

Left: Gold is found in rock called *ore*. The ore is heated to melt the gold. This man is pouring gold into ingots.

Right: A Zulu woman wears her festival headdress. The Zulus are the largest group of black Africans in South Africa.

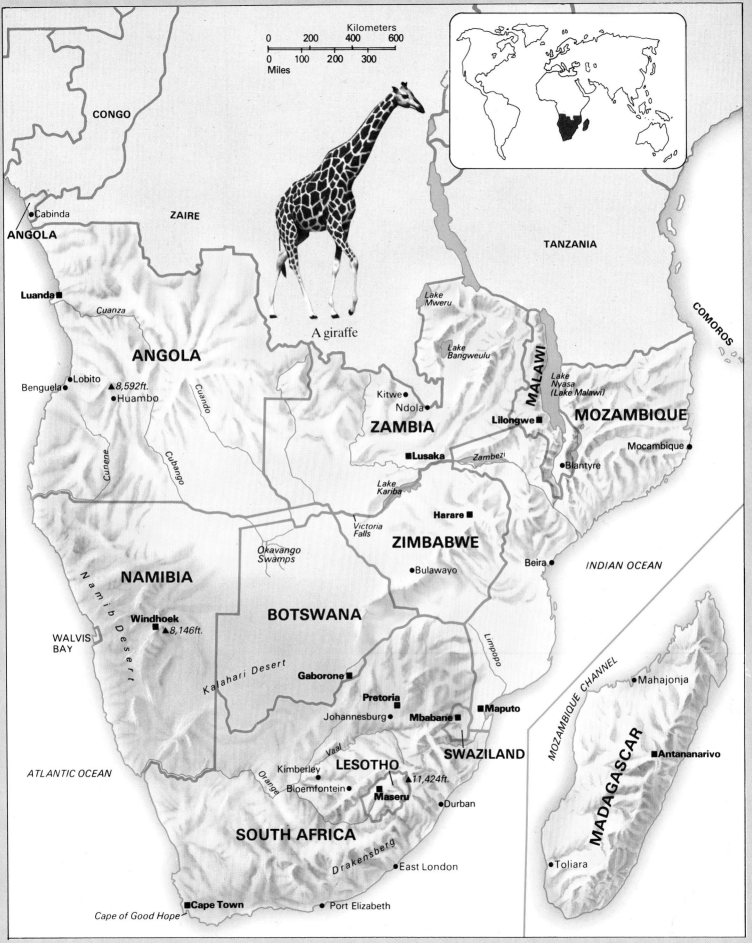

Kilometers
0   200   400   600

Miles
0   100   200   300

CONGO

ZAIRE

TANZANIA

Cabinda
ANGOLA

COMOROS

Luanda
Cuanza

Lake
Mweru

Lake
Bangweulu

MALAWI

Lake
Nyasa
(Lake Malawi)

ANGOLA

Benguela •Lobito
▲8,592ft.
•Huambo

Cuando

Cubango

Kitwe•
Ndola•

ZAMBIA

Lilongwe

MOZAMBIQUE

Mocambique•

Cunene

Lusaka

Zambezi

Blantyre•

Lake
Kariba

A giraffe

Harare

NAMIBIA

Windhoek
▲8,146ft.

Namib Desert

WALVIS
BAY

Okavango
Swamps

Victoria
Falls

ZIMBABWE

•Bulawayo

Beira•

INDIAN OCEAN

BOTSWANA

Kalahari Desert

Gaborone

Limpopo

MOZAMBIQUE CHANNEL

Mahajonja•

MADAGASCAR

Pretoria•
Johannesburg•

Mbabane•

Maputo

Antananarivo•

ATLANTIC OCEAN

Vaal

Kimberley•
Bloemfontein•

Orange

LESOTHO

▲11,424ft.
Maseru

SWAZILAND

•Durban

SOUTH AFRICA

Drakensberg

•East London

Toliara•

Cape Town
Cape of Good Hope

•Port Elizabeth

Australia

Australia is the largest island and smallest continent in the world. It is sometimes called "Down Under" because it lies south of the Equator among a group of islands in the Indian and Pacific Oceans.

Australia was discovered by Dutch sailors in the early 1600s. Much later, in 1770, Captain Cook took possession of parts of eastern Australia for Britain. At that time the Aborigines were the only people living there. Later, in the 1850s, gold was discovered and large numbers of settlers arrived from Europe in a hurry to make their fortunes. Today, besides gold, there are silver, copper, iron, zinc, and aluminum mines.

Much of the west of Australia is desert. Although it is a big country, it is not very crowded. Most people live in cities along the cooler southeast coast. In the dry, central plains called the "Outback," there are sheep and cattle stations. Sheep are kept mainly for their wool, which is sold to several other countries.

The Sydney opera house was built to look like the sailboats in the harbor. Sydney is the largest city in Australia.

A koala

Left: Ayers Rock rises high above the flat desert in the Northern Territory.

Below: Sheep stations cover much of the land west of the Great Dividing Range. These merino sheep are raised for their wool.

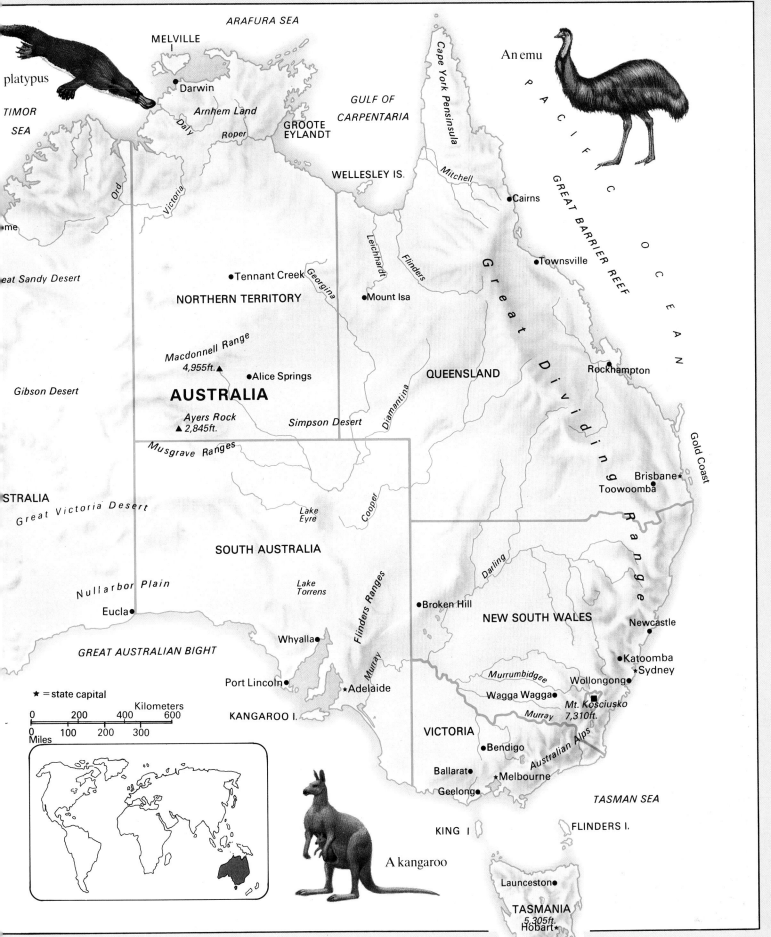

platypus

ARAFURA SEA

TIMOR SEA

MELVILLE I.

Darwin

Arnhem Land

Daly

Roper

Victoria

GROOTE EYLANDT

WELLESLEY IS.

GULF OF CARPENTARIA

Cape York Penisnsula

Mitchell

An emu

PACIFIC OCEAN

Cairns

GREAT BARRIER REEF

me

eat Sandy Desert

Ord

Tennant Creek

NORTHERN TERRITORY

Georgina

Leichhardt

Flinders

Mount Isa

Townsville

Gibson Desert

Macdonnell Range
4,955ft.▲

Alice Springs

AUSTRALIA

Ayers Rock
▲ 2,845ft.

Simpson Desert

Diamantina

QUEENSLAND

G r e a t   D i v i d i n g   R a n g e

Rockhampton

Musgrave Ranges

STRALIA

Great Victoria Desert

Cooper

Lake Eyre

SOUTH AUSTRALIA

Brisbane★
Toowoomba

Gold Coast

Nullarbor Plain

Eucla

Lake Torrens

Darling

Flinders Ranges

Broken Hill

NEW SOUTH WALES

Newcastle

GREAT AUSTRALIAN BIGHT

Whyalla

Murray

Murrumbidgee

Wagga Wagga

Katoomba
Sydney★
Wollongong

Port Lincoln

★Adelaide

Mt. Kosciusko
7,310ft.

★ = state capital

KANGAROO I.

Murray

Australian Alps

Kilometers
0   200   400   600

0   100   200   300
Miles

VICTORIA

Bendigo

Ballarat●

★Melbourne

Geelong●

TASMAN SEA

A kangaroo

KING I

FLINDERS I.

Launceston●

TASMANIA
5,305ft.
Hobart★

71

New Zealand and the Pacific

New Zealand and the islands of the Pacific Ocean are divided into three groups—Melanesia, Micronesia, and Polynesia—according to the type of people who live on the islands. Kiribati and the Caroline islands form part of Micronesia, but Fiji and Papua New Guinea are included in Melanesia.

New Zealand is part of Polynesia because the Maoris, the original inhabitants, are Polynesian people. New Zealand has two main islands, North Island and South Island. In the 1800s settlers arrived from Britain to farm and to prospect for gold. Today most people live in towns and cities and the largest city is Auckland. But New Zealand remains a rich farming country. Dairy farming is very important and there are over 9 million cattle and 55 million sheep. Many factory workers process meat, butter, cheese, and milk.

Life on the Pacific Islands is often relaxed and simple. Many islanders live in small villages. They grow food in gardens and fish skillfully from canoes. Others on larger islands work on banana, coconut, and cocoa plantations. Few islands have mineral resources, but phosphates are mined on Nauru and there are copper mines on Bougainville, one of the tiny islands that belongs to Papua New Guinea.

New Zealand   Fiji

Tonga   Kiribati

Tuvalu   Nauru

Vanuatu   Papua-New Guinea

Western Samoa   Solomon Islands

MARIANA ISLANDS (U.S.A.)

CAROLINE ISLANDS (U.S.A.)

IRIAN JAYA (INDONESIA)   PAPUA NEW GUINEA

Port Moresby

Coral Sea

AUSTRALIA

Above: An experienced sheep shearer can clip the wool from a sheep in less than thirty seconds.
Left: The island of Bora Bora in the Pacific is one of the Society Islands belonging to France. It was made by volcanoes and is mountainous. Other islands nearby are flat and made of coral. These islands are called *atolls*.

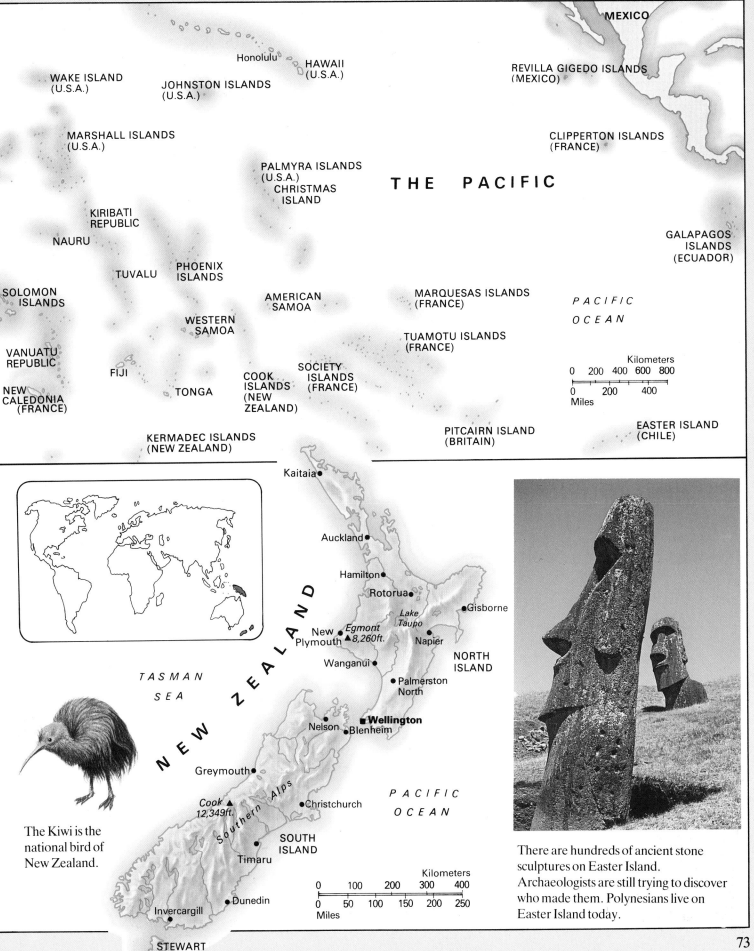

MEXICO

WAKE ISLAND
(U.S.A.)

JOHNSTON ISLANDS
(U.S.A.)

Honolulu

HAWAII
(U.S.A.)

REVILLA GIGEDO ISLANDS
(MEXICO)

MARSHALL ISLANDS
(U.S.A.)

CLIPPERTON ISLANDS
(FRANCE)

THE PACIFIC

PALMYRA ISLANDS
(U.S.A.)
CHRISTMAS
ISLAND

KIRIBATI
REPUBLIC

NAURU

GALAPAGOS
ISLANDS
(ECUADOR)

TUVALU

PHOENIX
ISLANDS

SOLOMON
ISLANDS

AMERICAN
SAMOA

MARQUESAS ISLANDS
(FRANCE)

PACIFIC

OCEAN

WESTERN
SAMOA

TUAMOTU ISLANDS
(FRANCE)

VANUATU
REPUBLIC

FIJI

COOK
ISLANDS
(NEW
ZEALAND)

SOCIETY
ISLANDS
(FRANCE)

Kilometers
0   200 400 600 800

NEW
CALEDONIA
(FRANCE)

TONGA

0   200   400
Miles

KERMADEC ISLANDS
(NEW ZEALAND)

PITCAIRN ISLAND
(BRITAIN)

EASTER ISLAND
(CHILE)

Kaitaia

Auckland

Hamilton

Rotorua

Gisborne

Lake
Taupo

New
Plymouth

Egmont
8,260ft.

Napier

NORTH
ISLAND

Wanganui

NEW ZEALAND

TASMAN

SEA

Palmerston
North

Wellington

Nelson

Blenheim

Greymouth

PACIFIC

Cook
12,349ft.

Southern Alps

Christchurch

OCEAN

SOUTH
ISLAND

The Kiwi is the
national bird of
New Zealand.

Timaru

Kilometers
0   100   200   300   400

0   50 100 150 250
Miles

Invercargill

Dunedin

STEWART
ISLAND

There are hundreds of ancient stone
sculptures on Easter Island.
Archaeologists are still trying to discover
who made them. Polynesians live on
Easter Island today.

The Polar Lands

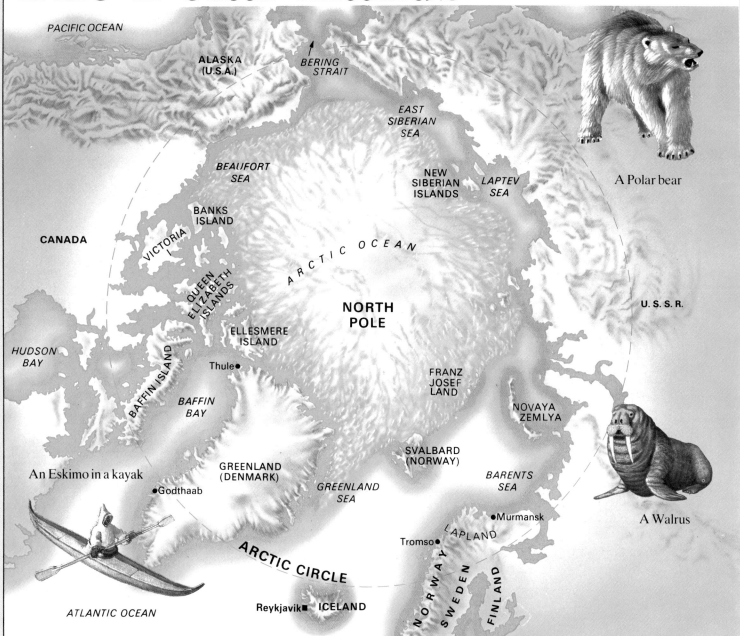

PACIFIC OCEAN

ALASKA (U.S.A.)

BERING STRAIT

EAST SIBERIAN SEA

BEAUFORT SEA

NEW SIBERIAN ISLANDS

LAPTEV SEA

BANKS ISLAND

CANADA

VICTORIA I

ARCTIC OCEAN

QUEEN ELIZABETH ISLANDS

NORTH POLE

ELLESMERE ISLAND

BAFFIN ISLAND

HUDSON BAY

Thule

FRANZ JOSEF LAND

U.S.S.R.

BAFFIN BAY

NOVAYA ZEMLYA

An Eskimo in a kayak

GREENLAND (DENMARK)

Godthaab

SVALBARD (NORWAY)

GREENLAND SEA

BARENTS SEA

Murmansk

A Walrus

Tromso

LAPLAND

ARCTIC CIRCLE

ATLANTIC OCEAN

NORWAY

SWEDEN

FINLAND

Reykjavik ■ ICELAND

A Polar bear

The Arctic

The area around the North Pole is called the Arctic. Much of it consists of the icy Arctic Ocean. But there are islands, including Greenland. Parts of North America, Europe, and Asia also stretch beyond the *Arctic Circle*. The waters around the North Pole are frozen all the year round. But in other parts of the Arctic the snow melts during the short summer weeks and patches of moss, lichen, and bright flowers appear. These areas are the Arctic *tundra*. Eskimos are the only people living in the Arctic. Most live on the southwest coast of Greenland and are skilled hunters and fishermen.

The Antarctic

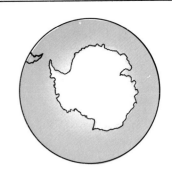

The continent of Antarctica covers almost 6 million square miles. It is larger than Europe and contains over 90 percent of the world's ice and snow. It is so bitterly cold in Antarctica that no one has ever lived there permanently. Whalers went there in the nineteenth century, but they never left the safety of their ships. Since 1911, when the South Pole was reached for the first time by Roald Amundsen, many scientists have been to the continent. They study the weather and the structure of the rocks buried in the ice. Research stations have been built there by a few countries, including the United States and the U.S.S.R.

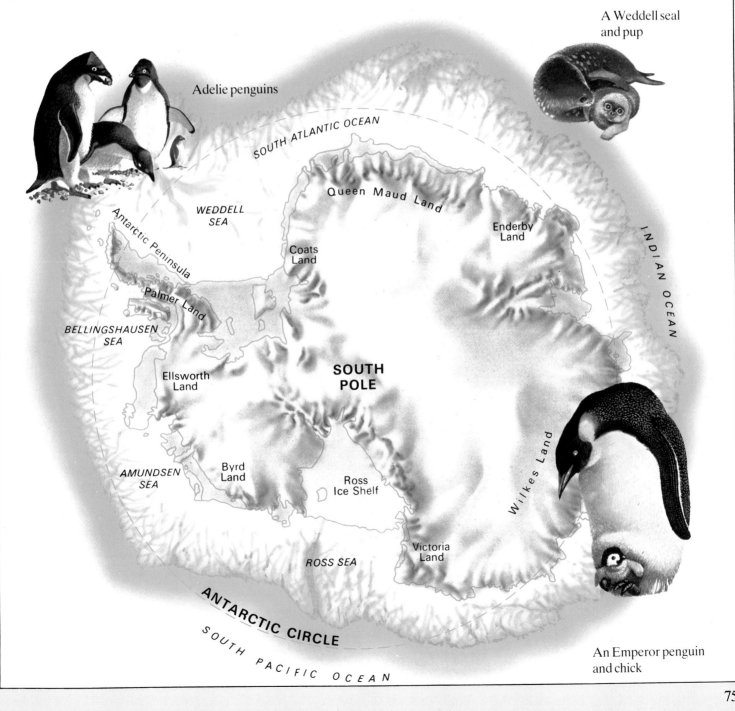

A Weddell seal and pup

Adelie penguins

SOUTH ATLANTIC OCEAN

Queen Maud Land

WEDDELL SEA

Enderby Land

Antarctic Peninsula

Coats Land

Palmer Land

INDIAN OCEAN

BELLINGSHAUSEN SEA

Ellsworth Land

SOUTH POLE

AMUNDSEN SEA

Byrd Land

Ross Ice Shelf

Wilkes Land

Victoria Land

ROSS SEA

ANTARCTIC CIRCLE

SOUTH PACIFIC OCEAN

An Emperor penguin and chick

Europe:
Facts and Figures

EUROPE

Country	Area (square miles)	Population	Capital	Official Language	Currency	Major Products
Albania	11,100	3,000,000	Tirane	Albanian	Lek	Oil, bitumen, metals (chrome, nickel, copper), tobacco, fruit, and vegetables
Andorra	175	32,700	Andorra la Vella	Catalan	French franc and Spanish peseta	Tourism, postage stamps
Austria	32,377	7,500,000	Vienna	German	Schilling	Food, iron and steel, textiles, paper products, machinery
Belgium	11,782	9,900,000	Brussels	Flemish, French	Belgian franc	Chemicals, vehicles, machinery, iron, steel
Bulgaria	42,826	8,900,000	Sofia	Bulgarian	Lev	Metals, machinery, textiles, tobacco, food
Czechoslovakia	49,377	15,500,000	Prague	Czech, Slovak	Koruna	Fuels, machinery, other manufactured goods, raw materials
Denmark	17,403	5,100,000	Copenhagen	Danish	Krone	Animals, meat, dairy produce, eggs, machinery, metals, and metal goods
Finland	130,129	4,900,000	Helsinki	Finnish, Swedish	Markka	Wood and wood pulp, paper, paperboard, machinery
France	211,223	55,000,000	Paris	French	French franc	Cars, electrical equipment, wine, cereals, textiles, leather goods, chemicals, iron, steel
Germany, East (German Democratic Republic—D.D.R.)	41,771	16,700,000	East Berlin	German	D.D.R. mark	Engineering goods, chemicals
Germany, West (Federal Republic of Germany)	95,983	61,000,000	Bonn	German	Deutschmark	Manufactured goods, chemicals, coke, consumer goods
Greece	50,948	10,100,000	Athens	Greek	Drachma	Manufactured goods, food, animals, wine, tobacco, chemicals
Hungary	35,922	10,800,000	Budapest	Hungarian	Forint	Transportation equipment, electrical goods, bauxite, aluminum, food, wine, pharmaceuticals
Iceland	39,771	200,000	Reykjavik	Icelandic	Krona	Fish products
Ireland, Republic of	27,138	3,600,000	Dublin	English, Irish	Irish pound (punt)	Meat and meat products, dairy products, beer, whiskey
Italy	116,322	57,400,000	Rome	Italian	Lira	Machinery, cars and trucks, iron and steel, textiles, footwear, plastics, fruit

Country	Area (square miles)	Population	Capital	Official Language	Currency	Major Products
Liechtenstein	60.6	26,000	Vaduz	German	Swiss franc	Cotton yarn and material, screws, bolts, needles
Luxembourg	999	400,000	Luxembourg	French, Luxemburgish (a German dialect)	Luxembourg franc	Iron and steel, chemicals, vehicles, machinery
Malta	122	400,000	Valletta	Maltese, English	Maltese pound	Food, manufactured goods, ship repairing, tourism
Monaco	0.7	25,000	Monaco	French	French franc	Tourism
Netherlands	15,771	14,500,000	Amsterdam; The Hague is the seat of government	Dutch	Guilder	Oil, chemicals, food and animals, machinery
Norway	125,191	4,200,000	Oslo	Norwegian	Krone	Animal products, paper, metals, metal products, fish, oil
Poland	120,734	37,300,000	Warsaw	Polish	Zloty	Lignite, coal, coke, iron and steel, ships, textiles, food
Portugal	35,556 (including Azores and Madeira)	10,400,000	Lisbon	Portuguese	Escudo	Textiles, timber, cork, machinery, chemicals, wine, sardines
Romania	91,706	22,800,000	Bucharest	Romanian	Leu	Food, machinery, minerals, metals, oil, natural gas, chemicals
San Marino	23.5	21,000	San Marino	Italian	Italian lira	Wine, cereals, cattle, tourism, postage stamps
Spain	194,912	38,600,000	Madrid	Spanish	Peseta	Manufactured goods, chemicals, textiles, leather goods, fish, wine, fruit and vegetables, olive oil
Sweden	173,245	8,300,000	Stockholm	Swedish	Swedish krona	Timber and timber products, machinery, metals and metal products, cars
Switzerland	15,943	6,500,000	Bern	French, German, Italian	Swiss franc	Tourism, machinery, chemicals and pharmaceuticals, watches, food, textiles
United Kingdom	94,535	56,400,000	London	English	Pound sterling	Manufactured goods, electrical and engineering products, transport equipment, textiles, chemicals, and plastics
U.S.S.R.	8,650,166	278,000,000	Moscow	Russian	Ruble	Iron, steel, chemicals, timber, paper, textiles (cotton), food, consumer goods
Vatican City State	0.17	1,000	Vatican City	Italian, Latin	Italian lira	
Yugoslavia	98,774	23,100,000	Belgrade	Serbo-Croat, Slovene, Macedonian	Dinar	Machinery, electrical goods, transportation equipment, chemicals

Asia:
Facts and Figures

ASIA

Country	Area (square miles)	Population	Capital	Official Language	Currency	Major Products
Afghanistan	250,018	14,700,000	Kabul	Pashtu, Dari	Afghani	Skins, cotton, natural gas, fruit
Bahrain	240	400,000	Manama	Arabic	Bahrain dinar	Oil
Bangladesh	55,602	101,500,000	Dacca	Bengali	Taka	Jute, leather, hide and skins, tea
Bhutan	18,148	1,400,000	Thimphu	Dzongkha	Ngultrum	Rice, fruit, timber
Brunei	2,226	200,000	Bandar Seri Begawan	Malay	Brunei dollar	Oil
Burma	261,237	36,900,000	Rangoon	Burmese	Kyat	Teak, oil cake, rubber, jute
Cambodia (Kampuchea)	69,903	6,200,000	Phnom Penh	Khmer	Riel	Rice, rubber
China	3,705,677	1,042,000,000	Beijing (Peking)	Chinese (Mandarin)	Yuan	Industrial and agricultural products
Cyprus	3,572	700,000	Nicosia	Greek, Turkish	Cypriot pound	Fruit, vegetables, wine, manufactured goods, minerals
Hong Kong	404	5,500,000	Victoria	English, Chinese (Cantonese)	Hong Kong dollar	Light manufactured goods, textiles, electronics
India	1,269,438	762,200,000	New Delhi	Hindi, English	Indian rupee	Tea, industrial goods, jute, textiles
Indonesia	782,720	168,400,000	Jakarta	Bahasa (Indonesian)	Rupiah	Oil, palm products, rubber, coffee
Iran	636,343	45,100,000	Tehran	Persian (Farsi)	Rial	Oil, natural gas, cotton
Iraq	167,937	15,500,000	Baghdad	Arabic	Iraqi dinar	Oil, dates, wool, cotton
Israel	8,020	4,200,000	Jerusalem	Hebrew, Arabic	Shekel	Cut diamonds, chemicals, fruit, tobacco
Japan	143,761	120,800,000	Tokyo	Japanese	Yen	Optical equipment, ships, vehicles, machinery, electronic goods, chemicals, textiles
Jordan	37,740	3,600,000	Amman	Arabic	Jordanian dinar	Phosphates, fruit, vegetables

Country	Area (square miles)	Population	Capital	Official Language	Currency	Major Products
Korea, North	46,543	20,100,000	Pyongyang	Korean	Won	Iron and other metal ores
Korea, South	38,028	42,700,000	Seoul	Korean	Won	Textiles, manufactured goods, chemicals
Kuwait	6,880	1,900,000	Al Kuwait	Arabic	Kuwaiti dinar	Oil, chemicals
Laos	91,436	3,800,000	Vientiane	Lao	Kip	Timber, coffee
Lebanon	4,016	2,600,000	Beirut	Arabic	Lebanese pound	Precious metals, gemstones
Macao	6.2	300,000	Macao	Portuguese, Chinese	Pataca	Light manufactured goods
Malaysia	127,326	15,700,000	Kuala Lumpur	Malay	Ringgit	Rubber, tin, palm oil, timber
Maldive Islands	115	200,000	Malé	Divehi	Maldivian rupee	Fish, copra
Mongolia	604,294	1,900,000	Ulan Bator	Mongol	Tugrik	Cattle, horses, wool, hair
Nepal	54,366	17,000,000	Katmandu	Nepali	Nepalese rupee	Grains, hides, cattle, timber
Oman	82,036	1,200,000	Muscat	Arabic	Omani riyal	Oil, dates, limes, tobacco, frankincense
Pakistan	310,427	99,200,000	Islamabad	Urdu	Pakistani rupee	Cotton, carpets, leather, rice
Philippines	115,839	56,800,000	Manila	English, Pilipino	Piso	Sugar, timber, coconut products
Qatar	4,247	300,000	Doha	Arabic	Qatar riyal	Oil
Saudi Arabia	830,060	11,200,000	Riyadh	Arabic	Saudi riyal	Oil
Singapore	224	2,600,000	Singapore	Malay, Chinese, Tamil, English	Singapore dollar	Refined oil products, electronic goods, rubber
Sri Lanka	25,334	16,400,000	Colombo	Sinhala	Sri Lanka rupee	Tea, rubber, coconut products, industrial goods
Syria	11,504	10,600,000	Damascus	Arabic	Syrian pound	Cotton, oil, cereals, animals

Country	Area (square miles)	Population	Capital	Official Language	Currency	Major Products
Taiwan	13,886	19,200,000	Taipei	Chinese (Mandarin)	Taiwan dollar	Textiles, electrical goods, plastics, machinery, food
Thailand	198,471	52,700,000	Bangkok	Thai	Baht	Rice, tapioca, rubber, tin
Turkey	301,404	52,100,000	Ankara	Turkish	Turkish lira	Cotton, tobacco, nuts, fruit
United Arab Emirates	32,280	1,300,000	Abu Dhabi	Arabic	Dirham	Oil, natural gas
Vietnam	127,252	60,500,000	Hanoi	Vietnamese	Dong	Fish, coal, agricultural goods
Yemen, North (Arab Republic)	75,295	6,100,000	San'a	Arabic	Riyal	Cotton, coffee, hides, and skins
Yemen, South (P.D.R.)	128,569	2,100,000	Aden	Arabic	Dinar	Cotton, fish, refined oil

North America:
Facts and Figures

NORTH & CENTRAL AMERICA

Country	Area (square miles)	Population	Capital	Official Language	Currency	Major Products
Antigua and Barbuda	171	100,000	St. John's	English	East Caribbean dollar	Oil products
Bahamas	5,381	200,000	Nassau	English	Bahamian dollar	Oil products
Barbados	166	300,000	Bridgetown	English	East Caribbean dollar	Sugar, oil products, electrical goods, clothing
Belize	8,867	200,000	Belmopan	English, Spanish	Belize dollar	Sugar, bananas, citrus products, fish, clothing
Canada	3,852,085	25,400,000	Ottawa	English, French	Canadian dollar	Wheat, natural gas, oil, wood pulp, newsprint, iron ore, cars and parts, fish
Costa Rica	19,577	2,600,000	San Jose	Spanish	Colon	Coffee, bananas, manufactured goods
Cuba	44,221	10,100,000	Havana	Spanish	Peso	Sugar, tobacco

Country	Area (square miles)	Population	Capital	Official Language	Currency	Major Products
Dominica	290	100,000	Roseau	English	East Caribbean dollar	Citrus fruits, bananas
Dominican Republic	18,818	6,200,000	Santo Domingo	Spanish	Peso	Sugar, coffee
El Salvador	8,125	5,100,000	San Salvador	Spanish	Colon	Coffee, cotton
Grenada	133	100,000	St. George's	English	East Caribbean dollar	Cocoa, nutmeg, mace, bananas
Guatemala	42,045	8,000,000	Guatemala City	Spanish	Quetzal	Coffee, bananas, cotton, beef
Haiti	10,715	5,800,000	Port-au-Prince	French	Gourde	Coffee, bauxite, sugar
Honduras	43,281	4,400,000	Tegucigalpa	Spanish	Lempira	Coffee, bananas, timber, meat
Jamaica	4,244	2,300,000	Kingston	English	Jamaican dollar	Bauxite, alumina
Mexico	761,166	79,700,000	Mexico City	Spanish	Peso	Oil, coffee, cotton, sugar, manufactured goods
Nicaragua	50,197	3,000,000	Managua	Spanish	Cordoba	Cotton, coffee, meat, chemicals
Panama	29,211	2,000,000	Panama	Spanish	Balboa	Bananas, shrimps, sugar, oil products
St. Christopher (St. Kitts) and Nevis	101	40,000	Basseterre	English	East Caribbean dollar	Sugar
St. Lucia	238	100,000	Castries	English	East Caribbean dollar	Bananas, cocoa, citrus fruits, coconuts, tourism, manufactured goods
St. Vincent and the Grenadines	150	100,000	Kingstown	English	East Caribbean dollar	Bananas, arrowroot, coconuts
Trinidad and Tobago	1,981	1,200,000	Port of Spain	English	Trinidad dollar	Oil, asphalt, chemicals, sugar, fruit, cocoa, coffee
United States	3,615,385	238,900,000	Washington D.C.	English	U.S. dollar	Machinery, vehicles, aircraft and parts, iron and steel goods, coal, chemicals, cereals, soya beans, textiles, cotton

South America:
Facts and Figures

SOUTH AMERICA

Country	Area (square miles)	Population	Capital	Official Language	Currency	Major Products
Argentina	1,068,379	30,600,000	Buenos Aires	Spanish	Peso	Meat and meat products, tobacco, textiles, leather, machinery
Bolivia	422,265	6,200,000	La Paz (seat of government); Sucre (legal capital)	Spanish	Peso	Tin, oil, natural gas, cotton
Brazil	3,286,727	138,400,000	Brasilia	Portuguese	Cruzeiro	Machinery, vehicles, soya beans, coffee, cocoa
Chile	295,754	12,000,000	Santiago	Spanish	Peso	Wood pulp, paper, copper, timber, iron ore, nitrates
Colombia	439,769	29,400,000	Bogota	Spanish	Peso	Coffee, emeralds, sugar, oil, meat, skins, and hides
Ecuador	109,491	8,900,000	Quito	Spanish	Sucre	Oil, bananas, cocoa, coffee
French Guiana	35,138	76,000	Cayenne	French	French franc	Bauxite, shrimps, bananas
Guyana	82,632	800,000	Georgetown	English	Guyanese dollar	Sugar, rice, bauxite, alumina, timber
Paraguay	157,059	3,600,000	Asunción	Spanish	Guarani	Cotton, soya beans, tobacco, timber
Peru	496,261	19,500,000	Lima	Spanish	Sol	Metals, minerals (silver, lead, zinc, copper), fish
Surinam	63,042	400,000	Paramaribo	Dutch, English	Guilder	Bauxite, alumina, rice, citrus fruit
Uruguay	68,042	3,000,000	Montevideo	Spanish	Peso	Meat, wool, hides, and skins
Venezuela	352,170	17,300,000	Caracas	Spanish	Bolivar	Oil, iron, cocoa, coffee

Africa:
Facts and Figures

AFRICA

Country	Area (square miles)	Population	Capital	Official Language	Currency	Major Products
Algeria	919,662	22,200,000	Algiers	Arabic	Algerian dinar	Natural gas, oil
Angola	481,389	7,900,000	Luanda	Portuguese	Kwanza	Coffee, diamonds, oil
Benin	43,487	4,000,000	Porto Novo	French	Franc C.F.A.	Cocoa, cotton
Botswana	231,822	1,100,000	Gaborone	English, Setswana	Pula	Copper, diamonds, meat
Burkina Faso	105,877	6,900,000	Ouagadougou	French	Franc C.F.A.	Livestock, groundnuts, cotton
Burundi	10,748	4,600,000	Bujumbura	French, Kirundi	Burundi franc	Coffee
Cameroon	183,583	9,700,000	Yaounde	English, French	Franc C.F.A.	Cocoa, coffee, oil
Cape Verde Islands	1,557	300,000	Praia	Portuguese	Escudo	Bananas, fish
Central African Republic	240,553	2,700,000	Bangui	French	Franc C.F.A.	Coffee, diamonds, timber
Chad	495,791	5,200,000	N'Djamena	French	Franc C.F.A.	Cotton, cattle, meat
Comoros	838	500,000	Moroni	French	Franc C.F.A.	Spices
Congo	132,057	1,700,000	Brazzaville	French	Franc C.F.A.	Oil, timber
Djibouti	8,495	300,000	Djibouti	French	Djibouti franc	Cattle, hides, and skins
Egypt	386,690	48,300,000	Cairo	Arabic	Egyptian pound	Cotton, oil, textiles
Equatorial Guinea	10,831	300,000	Malabo	Spanish	Ekuele	Cocoa, coffee, timber
Ethiopia	471,812	36,000,000	Addis Ababa	Amharic	Ethiopian dollar	Coffee, hides, and skins

Country	Area (square miles)	Population	Capital	Official Language	Currency	Major Products
Gabon	103,354	1,000,000	Libreville	French	Franc C.F.A.	Manganese, oil
Gambia	4,361	800,000	Banjul	English	Dalasi	Groundnuts
Ghana	92,106	14,300,000	Accra	English	Cedi	Cocoa, gold, timber
Guinea	94,971	6,100,000	Conakry	French	Syli	Alumina, bauxite
Guinea-Bissau	13,949	900,000	Bissau	Portuguese	Escudo	Fish, groundnuts
Ivory Coast	124,513	10,100,000	Abidjan	French	Franc C.F.A.	Cocoa, coffee, timber
Kenya	224,977	20,200,000	Nairobi	English, Swahili	Kenya shilling	Coffee, tea, hides
Lesotho	11,721	1,500,000	Maseru	English, Sesotho	Loti	Wool, mohair
Liberia	43,003	2,200,000	Monrovia	English	Liberian dollar	Iron ore, rubber
Libya	679,412	4,000,000	Tripoli	Arabic	Libyan dinar	Oil
Madagascar	226,674	10,000,000	Antananarivo	French, Malagasy	Malgache franc	Coffee, spices, vanilla
Malawi	45,750	7,100,000	Lilongwe	English, Chichewa	Kwacha	Tobacco, tea
Mali	478,801	7,700,000	Bamako	French	Mali franc	Groundnuts, cotton
Mauritania	397,984	1,900,000	Nouakchott	Arabic, French	Ouguiya	Iron ore, copper
Mauritius	805	1,000,000	Port Louis	English	Rupee	Sugar, tea, tobacco
Morocco	172,426	24,300,000	Rabat	Arabic	Dirham	Phosphates, fruit
Mozambique	302,352	13,900,000	Maputo	Portuguese	Metical	Sugar, fruit, vegetables
Namibia	318,284	1,100,000	Windhoek	Afrikaans, English	Rand	Minerals, diamonds, fish

Country	Area (square miles)	Population	Capital	Official Language	Currency	Major Products
Niger	489,227	6,500,000	Niamey	French	Franc C.F.A.	Groundnuts, livestock, uranium
Nigeria	356,695	91,200,000	Lagos	English	Naira	Oil, palm kernels, cocoa
Rwanda	10,170	6,300,000	Kigali	French, Kinyarwanda	Rwanda franc	Coffee
Sao Tome and Principe	373	100,000	Sao Tomé	Portuguese	Dobra	Cocoa
Senegal	75,756	6,700,000	Dakar	French	Franc C.F.A.	Groundnuts, phosphates
Seychelles	108	100,000	Victoria	English, French	Rupee	Copra, fish, spices
Sierra Leone	27,701	3,600,000	Freetown	English	Leone	Diamonds, iron ore
Somali Republic	246,219	6,500,000	Mogadishu	Somali	Somali shilling	Livestock
South Africa	471,479	32,500,000	Pretoria (seat of government); Cape Town (legal capital)	Afrikaans, English	Rand	Gold, diamonds, fruit, vegetables
Sudan	967,570	21,800,000	Khartoum	Arabic	Sudanese pound	Cotton, groundnuts
Swaziland	6,704	600,000	Mbabane	English	Lilangeni	Sugar, wood pulp, asbestos, fruit
Tanzania	364,927	21,700,000	Dodoma	English, Swahili	Tanzanian shilling	Coffee, cotton, sisal, spices
Togo	21,623	3,000,000	Lomé	French	Franc C.F.A.	Phosphates, cocoa, coffee
Tunisia	63,175	7,200,000	Tunis	Arabic	Tunisian dinar	Phosphates, olive oil, oil
Uganda	91,141	14,700,000	Kampala	English	Ugandan shilling	Coffee, cotton
Zaire	905,633	33,100,000	Kinshasa	French	Zaire	Coffee, cobalt, copper
Zambia	290,607	6,800,000	Lusaka	English	Kwacha	Copper
Zimbabwe	150,815	8,600,000	Harare	English	Zimbabwe dollar	Tobacco

Oceania:
Facts and Figures

THE PACIFIC

Country	Area (square miles)	Population	Capital	Official Language	Currency	Major Products
Australia	2,968,125	15,800,000	Canberra	English	Australian dollar	Cereals, meat, sugar, honey, fruit, metals and mineral ores, wool
Fiji	7,056	700,000	Suva	English, Fijian	Fiji dollar	Sugar, coconut oil
Kiribati	359	60,000	Tarawa	English, Gilbertese	Australian dollar	Copra, phosphates, fish
Nauru	8.1	8,000	Nauru	English, Nauruan	Australian dollar	Phosphates
New Zealand	103,744	3,400,000	Wellington	English	New Zealand dollar	Meat, dairy products, wool, fruit
Papua New Guinea	178,273	3,300,000	Port Moresby	English	Kina	Copra, cocoa, coffee, copper
Solomon Islands	10,984	300,000	Honiara	English	Solomon Islands dollar	Timber, fish, copra, palm oil
Tonga	270	100,000	Nuku'alofa	English	Pa'anga	Copra, bananas
Tuvalu	9.7	8,000	Fongafale	English, Tuvalu	Australian dollar	Copra
Vanuatu	5,700	100,000	Port Vila	Bislama, English, French	Vatu	Copra, fish
Western Samoa	1,097	200,000	Apia	English, Samoan	Tala	Copra, cocoa, bananas

General Index

Map Index

PHOTOGRAPHIC ACKNOWLEDGMENTS

The publishers wish to thank ZEFA for supplying the photographs for the cover and most of the photographs inside the book.

Additional photographs were supplied by J. Allan Cash (p. 9 *right*), Royal Netherlands Embassy (p. 17), British Tourist Board (p. 18 *top*), Renault (p. 20 *top right*), Italian Tourist Office (p. 28 *top*), Hungarian Tourist Office (p. 30 *bottom*), Greek Tourist Office (p. 33 *top*), Novosti (p. 34 *left*), Dave Collins (p. 38 *top right*), Sharp Electronics (p. 42 *top*), Thailand Tourist Board (p. 44 *top left*), New Jersey Travel and Tourism (p. 50 *right*), Rowntrees (p. 64 *right*), Satour (p. 68 *left* and *bottom*), Australian News and Information Bureau (p. 70 *left* and *top*), New Zealand Tourist Office (p. 72 *right*).